THE WHITE MONKS

The Cistercians in Britain 1128-1540

This book is dedicated to all my friends
who have helped me learn about the Cistercians
over the past twenty years,
my wife Denny, and children Hannah and Tomas
who now know more about the White Monks than is
probably good for them.
It is also dedicated to my dog, Mutt,
who knows many of the abbeys from his travels
in which he is always such excellent company.

THE WHITE MONKS

The Cistercians in Britain 1128-1540

Glyn Coppack

TEMPUS

First published 1998

Published by:
Tempus Publishing Limited
The Mill, Brimscombe Port
Stroud, Gloucestershire, GL5 2QG

Typesetting and origination by Tempus Publishing Ltd.
Printed and bound in Great Britain

British Library Cataloguing in Publication Data.
A catalogue record for this book is available from the British Library

ISBN 07524 1413 5

Contents

The illustrations

Text Figures

Colour plates (between 64 and 65)

Preface

The foundation of the 'New Monastery' of Cîteaux in 1098 began the most remarkable and successful religious movement of the Middle Ages. From unpromising beginnings in undrained marshland south of Dijon in France, a group of monks, who chose the white habit of reform, first inspired and then led by an English monk, St Stephen Harding, began a monastic family that spread across Europe. If Stephen Harding was the inspiration for the reform, it was St Bernard, the Burgundian abbot of Clairvaux, who was the organising genius who ran the order on military lines, dispatching colonies of White Monks, his 'New Soldiers of Christ', like a general deploying shock troops. Within 55 years, 339 monasteries of White Monks had been created across Europe, a number which rose to 525 by the end of the twelfth century. By the late seventeenth century the number of foundations had risen to 740.

In their earliest years, the White Monks were the fundamentalists of the monastic church, redefining religious life, liturgy, architecture, and art. Living literally off the land they were given, they brought about the first agricultural and industrial revolutions since the Roman occupation of Britain, and from the proceeds of these they built great monasteries, the ruins of many of which survive. Three of their churches remain in use, at Conwy, Holmcultram, and Abbey Dore. The buildings they are best known for are the great Yorkshire abbeys of Fountains, Rievaulx, and Byland, described by the twelfth-century historian William of Newburgh as the 'three shining lights of northern monasticism', jewels in the crown of any religious order. There were, however, 86 Cistercian monasteries in Britain established between 1128 and 1350, and of these more than half have surviving ruins or substantial earthwork remains. There were also some 32 Cistercian nunneries in England and Wales, with two churches that survive in use at Heynings and Swine. All were suppressed between 1536 and 1540.

The Cistercians, as the White Monks were formally called, came to Britain in 1128, only 30 years after the foundation of the abbey of Cîteaux itself, first settling at Waverley in Surrey. A second monastery at Tintern in 1131 and a third at Rievaulx in 1132 set the scene for the settlement of Britain, the first phase of which was completed within 20 years. The reform was spread by each of these new monasteries sending out colonies to settle new sites, mixing experienced monks with new recruits. Because the order worked to a template, in theory at least, every monastery was the same, with the same rules, the same books, and the same buildings. Reform, however, is not static, and what the Cistercian settlement of Britain shows is that the way the order's philosophy developed can be seen in the very variety of its buildings.

The Cistercians changed the landscape of Britain as their reform developed. Today, it is the ruins of their abbeys that provide the clearest indication of their existence, hauntingly beautiful buildings for the most part, set in dramatic countryside. Tintern, Rievaulx, Furness, Buildwas, Strata Florida, Valle Crucis, and Fountains are justly famous as much for the beauty of their settings as they are for their awe-inspiring buildings. We tend to forget, however, that when the Cistercians arrived these places were 'places thick-set with thorns, fit rather to be the lair of wild beasts than the home of men', real frontier territory where monks could seek communion with God away from the distractions of the world. It was the single-mindedness of the Cistercians that enabled them to take wild and inhospitable territory, tame it, and exploit it in a way that no other order managed. It was also their undoing – monks committed to poverty became rich and powerful as they first reclaimed and then developed marginal land, a power in the world they sought to avoid. It was, however, that wealth which gave us the buildings that remain and the landscape they are set in.

Although they were essentially an anti-intellectual order in their earliest years, the White Monks did appreciate the beauty of the countryside in which they set their monasteries. Abbot Bernard of Clairvaux wrote: 'You will find in woods something you will never find in books – stones and trees will teach you a lesson you never heard from the masters in the schools.' Abbot Aelred of Rievaulx, describing the Rye valley around his house found 'everywhere peace, everywhere serenity, and a marvellous freedom from the tumult of the world'. The names they gave their monasteries; Vaudey (the Valley of God), Strata Florida (the Valley of Flowers), Glenluce (the Valley of Light), Beaulieu (the Beautiful Place), Dieulacres (God's Field), and Abbey Dore (the Golden Abbey), show how much the Cistercians appreciated the places they developed.

If the abbeys themselves are the most obvious indications of the White Monks' presence, they are only a small part of the changes the Cistercians wrought on the countryside. Each abbey was largely self-sufficient, supported by a network of farms or granges. Vast acreages of marginal land were brought into cultivation for the first time since the pre-Roman Iron Age, cattle and sheep ranches created, and roads built. It is not for nothing that the land above Coniston is still called Furness Fells or the south flank of Pen-y-Gent is Fountains Fell and the land between Nidderdale and Colsterdale is Fountains Earth. Though no medieval farm buildings survive here, the landscape is still that of the cattle and sheep runs of Furness and Fountains which controlled these areas throughout the Middle Ages. Although the Cistercians are primarily remembered as sheep farmers, and it was wool that created their wealth, they practised a mixed economy that made most houses self-sufficient. The White Monks were farming innovators on a scale not seen again until the early nineteenth century, the monks developing their estates as single-mindedly as they built their monasteries and lived their lives. Avoiding the world outside the cloister, they had no qualms about evicting the occupants of villages displaced by either their monasteries or granges, and frequently went to law to protect the holdings they built up. They were not always scrupulous in their dealings, sometimes acquiring land by coercion or deception.

As well as being agricultural innovators, the Cistercians brought their organising skills to industry. From the late twelfth century, they invested heavily in metallurgy. Fountains, Rievaulx, Buildwas, and Bordesley in particular developed iron works at specialist granges. Fountains and Byland had extensive lead workings. Additionally, Byland had its own coal mines. Fountains operated its own potteries, and Meaux a tilery.

The appeal of the Cistercians today is a direct result of their success. Built in rural areas, many of their buildings survive and have been conserved for public enjoyment. Fountains, with over 300,000 visitors a year, is arguably the best-preserved medieval monastery in Europe. The landscapes they created survive in upland areas, areas which are easily accessible to hill walkers and ramblers. Both buildings and landscape are also easily accessible to scholars who have concentrated more of their energies on the Cistercians than any other religious order. Because of the White Monks centralised organisation, research in Britain produces results which are valid across Europe.

This book cannot pretend to be anything more than an introduction to the Cistercians and their monasteries in Britain. The subject is a vast one, and one that requires the skills of theologian, historian, architectural historian, historical geographer, sociologist, archaeologist, and surveyor. Consequently, much of the information I use is not my own, though any mistakes in its interpretation most certainly are. Much of the current Cistercian literature is out of date, and a considerable amount of recent research has yet to be published in full. I am indebted to many of my colleagues for keeping me up to date with their work and for pointing me in the right direction. First among these are Peter Fergusson, Stuart Harrison, David Robinson, Richard Fawcett, David Walsh, Sue Hirst, Susan Wright, Judith Roebuck, Keith Emerick, Mick Aston, Ron Shoesmith, Andrew Davison, Christopher Norton, and Terryl Kinder. None of them will be surprised to see that I have put my own gloss on their work and I am grateful for their forebearance. I also owe a huge debt of gratitude to English Heritage, which has over the past twenty years provided me with the opportunity to work on some of the finest Cistercian monasteries in Europe and supported my research on an international level. While this was not necessarily altruistic, the support I have been given went far beyond the day to day needs of the organisation itself. In particular, three people have supported my research and ensured that it was properly funded; John Hurst, Christopher Young, and Jeff West. That I could write this book at all is thanks to them. Perhaps even more important has been the help of my assistant, Jacqui Smith, who has performed the dual role of shielding me from distractions while I was working on the book and doing a lot of the basic seeking and finding of information. The ghost of Roy Gilyard-Beer, who first introduced me to the Cistercians in 1972, has been with me throughout the project, keeping me in line and making me think about what I have written. I am constantly aware that this is a book he should have written.

Glyn Coppack
Goxhill
January 1998

1 Who were the Cistercians?

The end of the first Christian millennium was widely expected to be the occasion of Christ's second coming, an awaited event that had a profound effect on the monastic church. Monks, after all, were men seeking God's kingdom on earth, and the anticipated coming of Christ's Kingdom was a pressing reason to put one's house in order. Their reaction caused them to examine critically the very roots of their traditions.

Across Europe, by the tenth century, most monastic communities had adopted a rule for communal life devised by St Benedict of Nursia for his community at Monte Cassino in Italy in the early years of the sixth century. The Benedictine rule, as it became known, provided a simple but consistent framework across cultures and national boundaries which brought together many communities which had little else in common. Indeed, all abbeys which adopted the rule were independent institutions, subject only to visitation by their local bishop. From the early years of the tenth century, and conveniently marked in 909 by the foundation a new abbey at Cluny near Mâcon in Burgundy, a strong reform movement began in the monastic church, aiming to root out corruption and standardise religious practices.

Cluny began its life as a Benedictine monastery, and benefited from a series of very able abbots who insisted on a stricter observanace of St Benedict's rule. The abbey was exempt from visitation by its local bishop, but was placed directly under the authority of the Pope. As it happens, the papacy was weak at the critical time that Cluny had strong abbots, and Cluny was able to function as a completely independent organisation. It was not long before Cluny became the centre of the reform movement, attracting many existing monasteries to re-found themselves on its model, and attracting the foundation of many new houses. All of these monasteries were in some way dependent on Cluny, though no Cluniac order existed in the tenth and eleventh centuries. As Cluny centralised, the abbey became the 'mother house' of a substantial family of subordinate monasteries, all of them priories, a completely new concept.

Cluny was one of the first monasteries not to be established in an isolated place, but in a lowland setting with room to plan and to expand. Its setting made it outward looking, and its 'family' of dependent houses made it rich and powerful. Central to the Cluniac reform was an insistence on the proper worship of God,

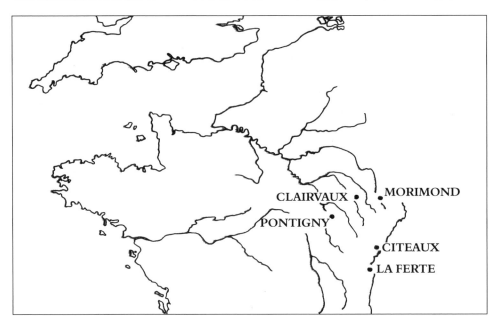

1   *Cîteaux and her daughter houses of La Ferté, Pontigny, Morimond, and Clairvaux.*

with the development of elaborate rituals and sumptuous buildings. St Benedict had required his monks to divide their lives into three parts: the saying of the church offices; spiritual reading and meditation; and manual labour. By 1090, so much time was taken up by the church offices at Cluny that manual labour had been abandoned and the monks had little opportunity to read and meditate. What had begun as a reform had stagnated.

Cluny, though, was not alone in its search for purity in monastic life, and St Benedict was not the only model to follow. The first monks had lived in the third and fourth centuries as virtual hermits in the deserts of Egypt, Palestine, and Syria, coming together only for protection and slowly developing a communal life. The 'desert fathers' provided an alternative approach that further separated monks from society, removing them from the corrupting influence of the world, and from the worldliness of the Benedictines and Cluniacs. The first appearances of 'desert' communities in Europe were the foundation of Camoldi in 1015 and Vallombrosa in 1039, both in northern Italy. These communities introduced a completely new class of illiterate quasi-monks, or lay brothers, enabling the monks themselves to be separated physically from the world. In 1084, St Bruno brought this concept to France, with the foundation of the Grande Chartreuse in the mountains of Dauphiné.

In 1098, a group of 20 or 21 monks led by Robert, the prior of the Cluniac monastery of Molesme, left that house to found a community that would return to the very roots of St Benedict's rule, incorporating some of the ideals of the desert fathers, and from very unpromising beginnings began what was to become the most spectacular and successful reform movement of the Middle Ages. They settled in a marsh 22.5km (14 miles) south of Dijon, and built a wooden monastery they called the New Monastery in 'a place of horror, a vast wilderness'. In Latin, the common monastic language, the site was called Cistercium (from cisterna, a marsh). In modern French it is called Cîteaux.

It was an Englishman, Stephen Harding, a monk of Sherborne in Dorset who had left the cloister and travelled widely, who had, according to William of Malmesbury writing his *Gesta Regum Anglorum* in 1122-23, fomented the dissent at Molesme that led to the founding of the New Monastery. Abbot Robert was forced to return to Molesme with half of his followers in 1099, and Harding finally became abbot in 1109, a post he was to hold until his death in 1135. His strict interpretation of the Benedictine rule, and particularly its insistence on poverty and manual labour, almost broke the community. Poor food, exhaustion, and the marshland setting of the monastery brought disease and death, though the convent's growing reputation for discipline and simple living was also its salvation. Cîteaux attracted patronage and many new recruits of exceptional ability, to the extent that a second monastery had to be established at La Ferté, in 1113. A third colony was established at Pontigny in 1114, and two more at Morimond and Clairvaux in 1115 (**1**). With Cîteaux, these four colonies were to become the core of the most successful monastic reform movement in the Middle Ages. By 1119, five more monasteries were established and the time had come formally to create a new Order.

The rapid growth of the New Monastery and her four daughter houses required the development of a monastic philosophy if the reform was to be maintained and strengthened. It was Stephen Harding who first codified the community's ideals, spiritual, social, and architectural. His approach was fundamental, going back to the earliest versions of St Benedict's rule, but also incorporating ideas first developed by St Basil (died 397) and John Cassian. Central to life at Cîteaux and her colonies were two documents: the Little Beginning (*Exordium Parvum*), an account of the origins of the order, and the Charter of Love (*Carta Caritatis*), an outline of the Cistercians' constitution. In its developed form, the *Exordium* is largely based on a lost account by Harding dating to about 1119 of the foundation of Cîteaux, though it contains material from the earliest years of the community. The *Carta Caritatis*, presented by Harding to Pope Calixtus II in 1119, was the constitution of the new order. Together they set an uncompromising insistence on poverty, simplicity of life, and the need physically to separate the community from the outside world. To prevent disturbance, new monasteries were to be placed 'far from the concourse of men', and were not to be dependent on cash revenues and feudal ties. They were not to own churches or mills because this brought them into contact with the outside world, but were to be self sufficient, and to farm the estates that supported them with lay brothers under monastic discipline. The rapid growth of the order stems as much from the opportunity it provided for the uneducated servant and working classes to enter religious life as to the discipline and strict standards that the choir monks set.

To ensure the stability of the Cistercian reform, the *Carta Caritatis* provided a model for a central authority within the order that remains a masterpiece of planning. Every year, every abbot was to attend a General Chapter at Cîteaux on 14 September, originally to provide an opportunity for the heads of all the communities to reaffirm their ties of love and mutual support but which rapidly developed to enforce collective discipline and to enact legislation by which the direction of the order could be controlled. Additionally, a cellular structure was created by which abbeys were arranged in families headed by Cîteaux and her four original colonies. Each new monastery was the responsibility of the abbey from which it was founded, and the abbot of that house was to visit annually the 'daughter house' to ensure it remained true to Cistercian principles. Papal consent was sought to free Cistercian monasteries from episcopal visitation to ensure that no outside influences could distract the Cistercian reform.

In common with other reform movements, the Cistercians chose a habit of undyed wool (Benedictine and Cluniac habits were black), and from this they rapidly became known as 'white monks' (**col. pl. 1**). Lay brothers wore a brown habit to distinguish them (**col. pl. 2**). Both were forbidden undershirts or breeches, an unheard of austerity in northern Europe. Their diet was sparse and unremittingly vegetarian, their lives were harsh and to a certain degree anti-intellectual, but they enjoyed 'everywhere peace, everywhere serenity, and a marvellous freedom from the tumult of the world'.

If Stephen Harding had created a model for monastic reform, it was Bernard of Clairvaux who provided the order with dynamism. As Bernard de Fontaine, a young Burgundian nobleman, he had entered Cîteaux in 1113 with a group of his followers. His progress from novice to the founding abbot of Clairvaux in less than three years was nothing short of remarkable, and as Bernard of Clairvaux he was eventually to replace Harding as the driving force of the order.

Bernard was a great organiser, planning the expansion of the order as a military exercise. Although he did not invent the expression, he directed the 'new soldiers of Christ' with military precision. Under his direction, Clairvaux began to outshine Cîteaux itself, and by his death in 1153, some 159 monasteries out of a total of 339 belonged to its filiation. He addressed himself to kings and princes, appealing strongly to the military classes he himself came from. He had no compunction about interfering with the running of his daughter houses, imposing abbots he knew he could trust and who would do his bidding without question, bringing to an already centralised order a degree of control that was exceptional.

He has been credited, probably wrongly, with the development of Cistercian architecture, the very framework of monastic life. Stephen Harding had rejected the distracting decoration of other orders, particularly in terms of furnishings and church plate. It was Bernard, however, who was to articulate the Cistercians' philosophy in this area. Writing to the Benedictine abbot William of St Thierry in the 1120s, he fulminated about the excesses of Cluniac building (**2**) and monastic

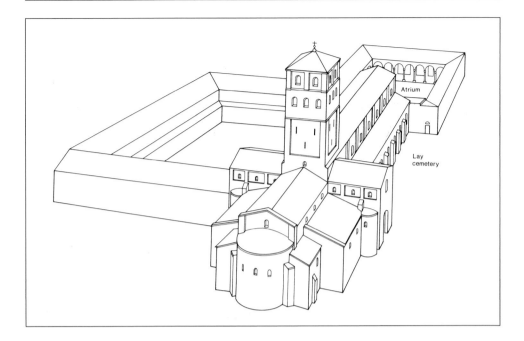

2   The abbey church of Cluny against which St Bernard took such exception (after Conant)

life. Particularly he dismissed 'the immense height of their churches, their immoderate length, their superfluous breadth, costly polishings and strange designs that, while they attract the eyes of the worshipper, hinder his attention'. At the time, his monastery of Clairvaux was built of wood and provided only the basics of monastic life (Chapter 2), and the Cistercians had not yet begun to build on the scale we see today. Indeed, early Cistercian communities were intentionally small, and as they grew with new recruits, the reform was spread by sending out new daughter houses. It was only since the building of a permanent monastery at Clairvaux between 1135 and 1145, a necessity that Bernard himself regretted, that a model existed for the 'Bernardine' church which has come to be accepted as the culmination of Bernard's architectural philosophy and the model for the surviving churches of the family of Clairvaux in Britain. Remarkably, it is Britain rather than Burgundy that has produced the evidence of the form and appearance of the earliest Cistercian monasteries.

The mission to Britain

The first Cistercian mission to England came from L'Aumône near Chartres in Normandy, a daughter house of Cîteaux, in 1128, and was established by William Giffard, Bishop of Winchester, close to his castle of Farnham in Surrey at Waverley. L'Aumône's second foundation was at Tintern in the borderlands of

3   Cistercian houses established in Britain before 1150.

Wales in 1131, on land provided by Walter fitz Richard, Lord of Chepstow, close to his castle. Nothing has been recorded of the process by which these two monasteries were established. They were, however, only the start of a remarkable phenomenon (**3**).

In 1131, however, Bernard of Clairvaux wrote to Henry I of England, who he had met early in that year: 'In your land there is an outpost of my Lord and your Lord, an outpost he has preferred to die for than to lose. I have proposed to occupy it and am sending men from my army who will, if it is not displeasing to you, claim it, recover it, and restore it with a strong hand.' Behind this letter were the actions of Walter Espec, Lord of Helmsley and a Royal Justiciar, a vassal of both King Henry and King David I of Scotland. He had offered St Bernard a site in the valley of the Rye to the west of Helmsley, and the emissaries sent from Clairvaux were to inspect the new site and report back on its suitability. Espec had already sought the support of both his feudal lords and Thurstan, the reformist Archbishop of York, and in March 1132, a group of 12 Clairvaux monks, many of them Yorkshiremen, led by Abbot William, a scholar from York who had served as Abbot Bernard's secretary, were formally settled at Rievaulx. The foundation of Rievaulx Abbey was carefully planned, not just to take the Cistercian mission to England, but also to Scotland, and in this, St Bernard's hand can be plainly seen.

The arrival of the Cistercians in Yorkshire had a dramatic effect. Passing through York, the White Monks had come to the attention of many members of the Benedictine York Abbey. Six monks there, Ranulf, Thomas, Gamel, Hamo, Walter, and Gregory, and the sacrist, Richard, began to press for reform of their own community. Abbot Geoffrey of York was not prepared to have his authority questioned or his abbey reformed, and the community was split. The prior, another Richard, the sub-prior Gervase, Geoffrey, Robert of Subella, Radulf, Alexander, and Robert, a former monk of Whitby, joined the dissenters, and Archbishop Thurstan became aware of the dissent. On 6 October 1132 he carried out a visitation of York Abbey in attempt to resolve the issue, but Abbot Geoffrey, supported by other Benedictine abbots and Cluniac priors, stood his ground. When the archbishop arrived, there was a brawl in the cloister as the monks tried to prevent his officials entering the chapter house. Thurstan had little choice but to place York Abbey under an interdict, and to take the dissenters into his own protection. On 27 December 1132, Fountains Abbey was established for this group in the valley of the Skell to the west of Ripon, and in the following year the community petitioned for acceptance in the Cistercian order and sought guidance from Abbot Bernard. In this way, Clairvaux acquired by adoption a second daughter house in Yorkshire.

Clairvaux' interest in England did not end with the establishment of Fountains, however. In 1143, a third daughter house was established at Boxley in Kent with the support of William de Ypres, son of the Count of Flanders. Wales was also fertile ground for Clairvaux, with the establishment of Whitland Abbey in 1140 with the support of Bernard, Bishop of St Davids, and Margam Abbey in 1147 on land given by Robert, Earl of Gloucester. Both were, however, intended to bolster English power in Wales.

The means by which the Cistercian reform was spread was the foundation of daughter houses, each of which required an abbot, normally one of the senior monks of the founding community, 12 choir-monks, and an unknown number of lay brothers. Thus, the rate at which daughter houses could be established was dependent not only on patronage, but also on the growth of the mother community. Support for the White Monks in the first half of the twelfth century came from two sources: the established non-monastic church, and the great baronial families, people who had previously supported an earlier wave of monastic reform, the Augustinian canons. In Britain, it tended to be those who had done well from the patronage of Henry I. Although it was Bishop Giffard who first brought the Cistercians to Britain, he was followed in four years by Archbishop Thurstan of York at Fountains; in 1137 by Bishop Alexander 'the Magnificent' of Lincoln who was patron of both Thame and Louth Park in that year, and Bishop Bernard of St Davids settled Whitland three years later. Walter Espec, the founder of Rievaulx, was a friend and courtier of Henry I; King David of Scotland, who brought the Cistercians to Melrose in 1136, was brought up in Henry I's court; and the aristocracy represented in the first wave of foundations comprised the likes of Robert de Beaumont, earl of Leicester, his brother Waleran de Meulan, earl of Worcester, William de Roumare, earl of Lincoln, and Simon de Senlis, half-brother of King David of Scotland, all leading members of the King's court. The Cistercians had attracted the support of the most powerful men in Britain.

The process of founding a daughter house was a fairly slow one, if the example of Kirkstead can be taken as typical. Hugh Brito, Lord of Tattershall in Lincolnshire, had visited Fountains in 1137, offering a site for a new monastery on the northern edge of the fen. The offer was accepted and brother Adam was dispatched to survey the site and to erect wooden buildings for the community. It was two years, however, before a founding community was sent out to settle the site. The order's statutes required that, in addition to the necessary buildings, a new monastery should have its full complement of necessary and approved books, a missal, a copy of the Gospels, a gradual, an antiphonary, a hymnal, a psalter, a copy of the rule, and a religious calendar. Since these books had to conform with Cistercian orthodoxy they would have to be laboriously copied from Fountains' own collection of approved books. When Robert of Subella, one of the founding community of Fountains, settled with his brothers at Kirkstead he had everything he needed to begin the full round of monastic life, his situation cloned from that of the mother community.

2 The Cistercians' earliest buildings

Because the Cistercians wanted to return to the simplicity of the Benedictine rule it is hardly surprising that they rejected the developed architecture of the Benedictines and Cluniacs in favour of a simplified framework for religious life. They reduced the standard monastic plan exemplified since the early ninth century by the schematic plan of the Swiss monastery of St Gallen to the bare minimum required for religious life.

Before 1113, the order had legislated that no new community could be established 'without the prior construction of such places as an oratory, a refectory, a dormitory, a guest-house, and a porter's cell, so that the monks may immediately serve God and live in religious discipline'. This was what had been provided at Cîteaux in 1098 where the first White Monks had cleared the site and built, with the help of Odo, Duke of Burgundy, a timber monastery. It was in such a house at Clairvaux that St Bernard had written to William of St Thierry in c1124 fulminating against the pride and excesses of Cluniac architecture, and it was from Clairvaux in 1131 that the architect-monk Geoffrey of Ainai came to England to lay out the first timber buildings at Rievaulx to house the community that settled there in March 1132 .

Simple wooden monasteries

Although the Cistercians had abandoned the formal cloister layout of Benedictine and Cluniac monasteries as they searched for a framework more compatible with St Benedict's rule, it took almost a generation to decide what the appropriate form of their buildings would be, a process which was only being completed as the White Monks began to settle in Britain. Both Cîteaux and Clairvaux retained their timber buildings in the early twelfth century, but their replacement in stone was beginning.

Timber buildings were, by their very nature, temporary and were normally intended to serve only until a monastery had reached a state of social and financial stability. They were not only the preserve of the Cistercians, for they have been identified on such diverse sites as the Augustinian priory of Norton in Cheshire and the Carthusian charterhouse of Mount Grace in Yorkshire. In the context of the familial relationships between Cistercian monasteries, however, they

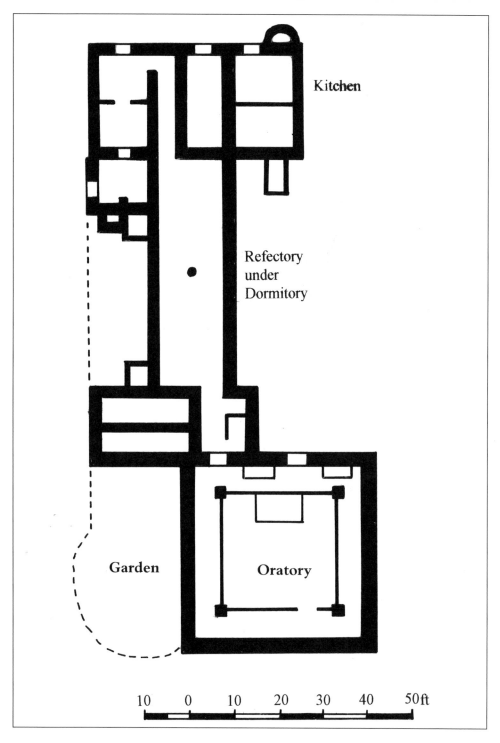

Kitchen

Refectory
under
Dormitory

Garden

Oratory

10 0 10 20 30 40 50ft

4   The first monastery of Clairvaux, from which Geoffrey of Ainai came to lay out the first buildings at
Rievaulx and Fountains (after Milley).

demonstrate an orthodoxy which implies deliberate planning. Such buildings are regularly referred to in contemporary documents as built 'according to the form of the order' or 'after our custom'. If this is true, it would appear that as much attention was paid to the form of buildings as to the provision of approved books and the simplified plainsong that marked Cistercian worship. While books survive from this period, no timber buildings survive in Britain. Indeed the only early Cistercian buildings to survive, partly remodelled, are the remains of the first monastery at Clairvaux (**4**). These buildings, described by visitors to the abbey in 1517 and 1667, comprised an enclosure with a small timber chamber near the gate, apparently used by guests, containing a square timber church and a two-storey domestic building 15m long that comprised the refectory at ground level and dormitory at first floor. A small kitchen lay close by. There was no chapter house or cloister, and the buildings accord exactly with the early requirements of the order. Timber buildings may not survive elsewhere, but they are well known in Britain and elsewhere from two sources: near contemporary Cistercian chronicles and excavation.

In Britain, the best evidence comes from the family of Fountains Abbey. In about 1206, Abbot John of York commissioned Hugh, a monk of Kirkstall, to write the approved history of the foundation and early years of Fountains before it was lost to memory. To achieve this, Hugh was to make use of the recollections of Serlo, then 99 years old and a monk of Kirkstall, who had been at Fountains from 1137 to 1147, and to consult other sources where Serlo's memory had faded. The account which is not strictly history in the modern sense, is strongly coloured by the writer's Cistercian indoctrination, and shows a remarkable vagueness about dates. Serlo himself was unconcerned about buildings, and had little concept of time; he was also recounting a story many elements of which would not be remarkable to a Cistercian audience and were thus not worth repeating. He, or Hugh, sought parallels for what had occurred in the Old Testament, and the story that was finally told may well have been slightly modified to fit the quotations taken so freely from the Vulgate Bible. His interest lay in the hardships faced by the early community, their faith, and the spread of the Cistercian mission. All the same, the history recorded in the early thirteenth century has proved where it can be checked by excavation to be remarkably accurate.

The community who settled at Fountains were not Cistercians but a group of dissident Benedictines from York Abbey who had been removed to Skelldale for their own safety in December 1132. After a desperate winter sheltering in caves and below an elm tree they sent a message to Clairvaux seeking help and admittance to the order. Abbot Bernard responded by sending Geoffrey of Ainai, recently returned from Rievaulx, to advise the new community. Geoffrey was described as an old man who was regularly used by St Bernard to assist in setting up new communities, especially those converting to the Cistercian rule, a monk skilled both in Cistercian life and buildings. By the early summer of 1134, carpenters were present at Fountains and the building of a timber monastery had begun. Perhaps more important, Geoffrey passed his skills on to two members of the Fountains community, Adam and Robert who had joined the community in 1133, and who are the only monks named in the Fountains chronicle as responsible for setting up new daughter houses. Presumably he had done the same at Rievaulx though the lack of a chronicle there means we will never know. In the Fountains family, brother Adam was the most active in this field, setting out new monasteries at Kirkstead in 1139, at Woburn in 1145, at Vaudey in 1147, and at Meaux in 1151, where he became the first abbot. Brother Robert became the first abbot of Fountains' first daughter house of Newminster in Northumberland, where he was credited with 'setting out the buildings therein after our manner. At Barnoldswick, settled in 1147, lay-brothers from Fountains raised buildings 'according to the form of the order', though we are not told who was responsible for them, and when this house was resettled at Kirkstall in 1152, Abbot Alexander (sometime prior of Fountains) 'elevated a basilica . . . and arranged humble buildings according to order'. Here, the use of the word *basilica* implies a masonry church; otherwise, the first buildings were again of timber.

The chronicle of Meaux Abbey, written by the nineteenth abbot Thomas Burton at the end of the fourteenth century using earlier sources that do not survive, describes the earliest buildings there in some detail. William of Aumâle, the founder, raised 'a certain great house built with common mud and wattle . . . in which the arriving lay brothers would dwell until better arrangements were made for them. He also built a certain chapel next to the aforementioned house . . . where all the monks used the lower storey as a dormitory and the upper to perform the divine service devoutly.' These buildings proved to be too small and Abbot Adam replaced the first-floor oratory and ground-floor dormitory with a larger wooden building of the same form, suggesting that the layout was 'according to the form of the order', though it differed substantially from the layout of the first timber buildings at Fountains. Other offices, presumably the missing refectory, guest-house, and porter's cell were also built, using timber from the demolished castle of Montferant, though they are not described in any detail. The combination of dormitory and oratory in a single building has long been thought to be strange, but Adam was too experienced in Cistercian orthodoxy to oversee buildings which were not in accordance with the rule and legislation of the order. Presumably, the form and layout of buildings was still being developed.

Outside the family of Fountains, evidence for the form of the first Cistercian houses in Britain is slight. Monks from Waverley settled at Thame in Oxfordshire in 1138 in buildings provided by the patron Robert Gait on a site provided by Bishop Alexander of Lincoln, as was the norm. That buildings might be supplied by a patron without supervision from a founding abbey is apparent from only one case. At Pipewell in Northamptonshire, William Batevileyn provided a site and temporary buildings which he offered to both Garendon Abbey and Newminster. Founding communities were dispatched from both houses, suggesting that neither knew of the other's interest, a remarkable occurrence in an order as centralised as the Cistercians. It also suggests that neither had provided

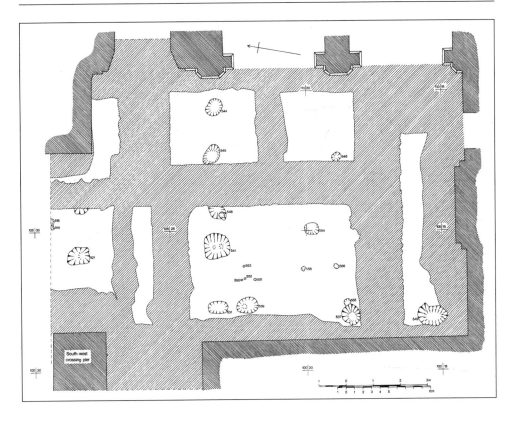

5   *Plan of the first timber buildings at Fountains. The church is represented by two lines of post-holes on the left of the plan, the domestic building lies to the right. Only its east wall has been excavated.*

supervision of the building. Eventually, the Garendon monks withdrew leaving Pipewell to join, through Newminster, the family of Fountains.

The evidence of excavation goes some way to establishing just what the documentary evidence means. Three sites have produced evidence in recent years of substantial timber buildings belonging to the foundation period, at Fountains and its grand-daughter house of Sawley founded in 1147, and Bordesley, founded in 1138 from Garendon, a grand-daughter house of Waverley. In each case, the evidence is incomplete and slightly contradictory, but one should remember that the order's philosophy of building was developing rapidly and the sites are not necessarily contemporary.

At Fountains, the principal buildings laid out to the instructions of Geoffrey of Ainai in 1134 have been recovered by excavation below the later abbey church (**col. pl. 3**) and comprise the oratory or church and a domestic building (**5**). Both were built of squared timber, suggesting that they were sophisticated carpentered structures, and were roofed with shingle or thatch. The oratory lay east to west and was a plain rectangular building at least 10.5m long and 4.8m wide. Both its gable walls had been destroyed when the standing church was built. Double post-pits in its western surviving bay indicated shallow porches and doors in both the north and south walls, suggesting that the building only extended another bay to the west. The domestic building is known only from its east wall, three deep post holes that represented a surviving wall 8m long. The construction of the south transept gable of the standing church had removed south end of the wall but no trace of this building was seen in excavation to the south. It can have been no longer than 12m, slightly smaller than the contemporary domestic building at Clairvaux, and its width is unknown. Because its post holes were deeper than those of the church, it is presumed to have had two storeys, the refectory at ground-floor level and dormitory above. Because the buildings were so close together and overlapped slightly, a stair from the dormitory into the church is likely. These buildings remain the earliest Cistercian buildings to have been identified on the ground in Britain, though slightly earlier structures are known to have existed at Rievaulx, for the timber guest-house there which caught fire in 1134 is described in Walter Daniels's Life of Aelred written in the 1170s, and must have existed at both Waverley and Tintern.

Excavation at Bordesley, though extensive, has failed to locate identifiable temporary buildings below the later church, though it is not unusual for stone buildings to be erected in areas away from temporary buildings that remain in use. At Clairvaux, the permanent stone monastery begun in 1135 was sited some distance to the east to avoid disturbing the community during building. All the same, a series of early graves in the monks' cemetery were covered with reclaimed timbers from demolished buildings, one of which has produced a felling date of 1141-59 quite consistent with the erection of temporary buildings after the foundation of the house in November 1138. The Cistercians of Signy in the Ardennes chose symbolically to bury the timber that could not be reused from their temporary buildings when they replaced them with permanent structures; such was the attachment of the founding community at Bordesley that they took fragments to their graves.

Sawley Abbey was established in Craven in 1148, the third daughter house of Newminster, at the behest of Abbot Robert, one of the Fountains monks trained by Geoffrey of Ainai. Excavation below the south side of the cloister and within the latrine block has revealed a series of no less than five timber buildings that predate the building of a stone abbey (**6**). One would expect that these buildings would be raised 'after our custom'. The earliest, Buildings A and B dated from the period of settlement and like the Fountains buildings before them had earth-fast posts. Here, though, the similarity ended, for where the carpenters at Fountains had set squared posts in straight lines to frame the walls of their buildings, at Sawley the posts were left untrimmed and imperfectly aligned. In fact, they point to a different building tradition, earth walls with timber stiffening, a technique well known in the north of England.

Building A (**7**) was a building some 6.8m wide and more than 17.7m long, aisled in at least six bays. The slightly irregular positioning of the arcade posts

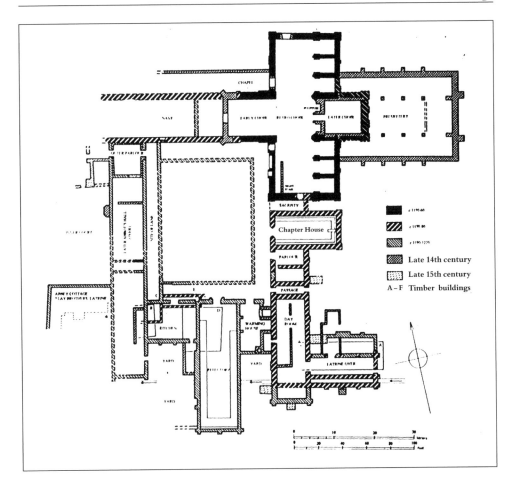

Sawley Abbey, showing the location of the timber buildings A to E on the south side of the cloister.

indicates a method of construction known as 'reverse assembly'. The door was located in the third bay of the south wall and it was provided with an internal porch, a provision which suggests that this was a domestic building. Although the building does not appear to have been of sophisticated construction it was probably no poorer in its construction than a manorial hall in its locality and there is no reason to expect that its walls were not cleanly finished and plastered, and its roof covered with graduated slates, some of which were recovered in excavation. Its floor was cobbled. Most remarkably, this building was supplied with a piped water supply. A lead pipe, laid in clay in a stone conduit, ran from outside the building to the narrow fifth bay of the south aisle where the must have been a tap. At this point, a soak-away was provided to take waste water. This building, which had evidence of lead working in its north aisle, had been repaired at least once

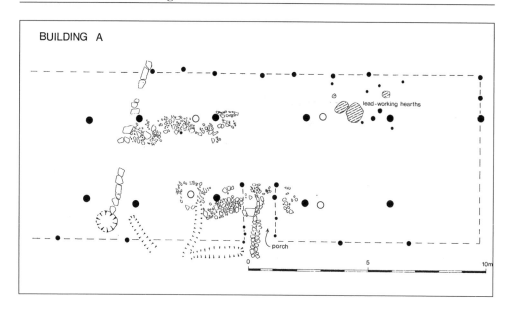

BUILDING A

lead-working hearths

porch

0   5   10m

7   *Building A at Sawley Abbey, an aisled building with clay walls built about 1150 and perhaps used by*
the lay brothers in the earliest years of the monastery. Building B was a similar structure.

before it was demolished in the 1160s. It looks very much like the first building
raised at Meaux for the lay-brothers only a year or two later, even in its
construction, and given the building sequence at Sawley, probably served the same
purpose, their dormitory and refectory, turned over as required for industrial use.
Building B (**8**) was also 6.8m wide, though of unknown length, and probably
aisled. It too had a piped water supply, but its use is unknown. Both these
buildings were contemporary with the construction of a stone church which from
its detailing must have been started in 1148, and it is possible that no temporary
church was provided. Perhaps Sawley followed the same model as Kirkstall with
its basilica and humble offices built only four years later.

    What is particularly valuable about the timber buildings at Sawley is that they
continued in use throughout a period of some 50-60 years as the permanent
monastery was built and they show a development which is seen nowhere else. In
the 1160s, three new buildings (**8**) were raised to house a growing community.
The first, Building C, was a replacement for Building B, aligned north to south
rather than east to west like its predecessor. This was a properly carpentered
building, its principal posts set on pad-stones, an improvement on the earth-fast
joinery of the previous generation. Between the pad-stones, rubble footings
supported cill-beams that carried the panels of the walls. It had a cobbled floor,
and like its predecessor was supplied with piped water. Butted against its east wall
was a second building, E, represented only by the pad-stones and footings for the
interrupted cills of its south wall and a large area of its mortar floor. In the angle

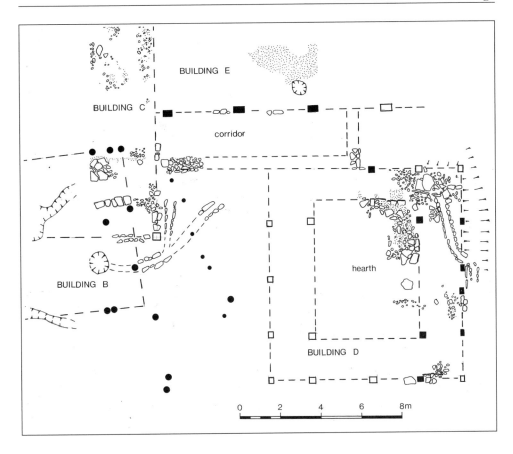

8   *Buildings C, perhaps the guest hall, D, the kitchen, and E, perhaps the refectory and dormitory of the timber monastery at Sawley in the 1160s and 70s.*

formed by these two structures was Building D, a fully carpentered kitchen some 10m square, aisled on all four sides and with a central hearth. This was the most sophisticated building recovered at Sawley and the earliest monastic kitchen to have been excavated. The kitchen had its own water supply, and a large sink in its north-east corner. Towards the end of its life, perhaps in the 1170s, it was linked to Buildings C and E by a stone-walled corridor.

As a stone church had been provided earlier, the only major buildings required by Cistercian statute at this date are a refectory, a dormitory, and a guest-house. The first and last of these would necessarily be associated with a kitchen. Following the Fountains model (which itself follows Clairvaux) the dormitory and refectory would have occupied the first and ground floors of the same building, in this case the more substantial Building E. Building C could easily be a guest hall.

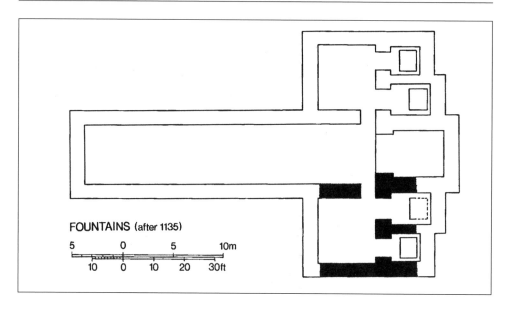

9 *Reconstructed plan of the first stone church at Fountains Abbey completed before 1146.*

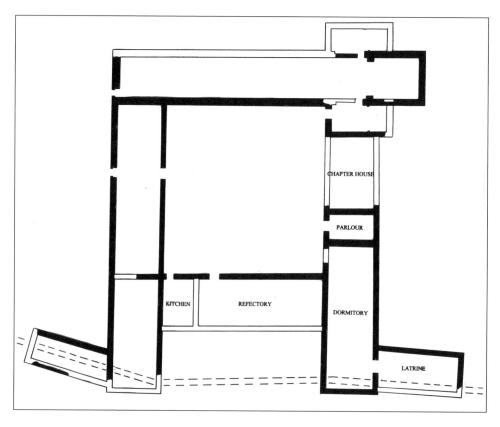

10 *The first stone monastery at Waverley, built in the early 1130s (after Brakspear).*

The first stone monasteries

Building in stone followed as soon as a monastery achieved stability, that is as soon as it acquired sufficient monks, lay brothers, and endowment to ensure its survival. Once again, the form of the buildings was strictly laid down and any community which began to build in contravention of the strict rules of the order was firmly brought into line by the General Chapter. It was not unknown for communities to be instructed to demolish offending buildings, as indeed happened at Meaux in 1160.

Very few of the earliest Cistercian abbeys have survived in Britain or on the Continent, but sufficient has been recovered by excavation and the study of surviving fabric at Waverley, Tintern, Melrose, and Fountains to establish their form. Recent research has also started to reveal the earliest stone buildings at Rievaulx. None is earlier than the replanning of Clairvaux in 1135, when the monastery there was rebuilt by Achard assisted by Geoffrey of Ainai and completed by 1145. At Fountains, the principal builder was Henry Murdac, a Yorkshireman who was a close confidant of St Bernard and who had been responsible for the building in stone of the abbey of Vauclair on the Somme. He had been imposed on Fountains to ensure Cistercian orthodoxy in 1144, and that must also have been the orthodoxy of St Bernard himself. Waverley, however, belonged to the family of Cîteaux, as did Tintern, both being daughter houses of L'Aumôme. Here, Bernard's influence need not have been so great. There is, however, a consistency which suggests that the Cistercians had already fixed their architectural philosophy. Interestingly, the plan form adopted was a modified version of the Benedictine plan, a plan which had initially been abandoned by the Cistercians.

The first stone church at Fountains (**col. pl. 3**) had been built in 1136, a small building with a short square presbytery, transepts with two eastern chapels (**5**), and a short unaisled nave. To this early church, Murdac added an extended aisled nave of nine bays that was exactly the same length and width as the nave of the church he had just completed at Vauclair. Only the south transept and part of the presbytery and crossing have been excavated, but sufficient has been seen to be fairly sure about its form and elevation (**9, 14**). It had been damaged by a recorded fire in 1146 and repaired, preserving the blue, red, and green glass from some of its windows and fallen wall plaster that was painted a pale pink below its new floors. The nave and transepts had an earth floor, though the presbytery and transept chapels had better quality mortar floors. The floor in the quire was strewn with rushes. The general impression was one of dignified simplicity, though the coloured window glass does not accord with the Cistercian requirement for plain glass that was certainly current by 1139 when a plan to convert the Augustinian priory of Kirkham required the replacement of its coloured windows with plain glass.

At Waverley, almost the complete layout of the first stone church and cloister ranges was determined by excavation (**10**) at the beginning of this century by

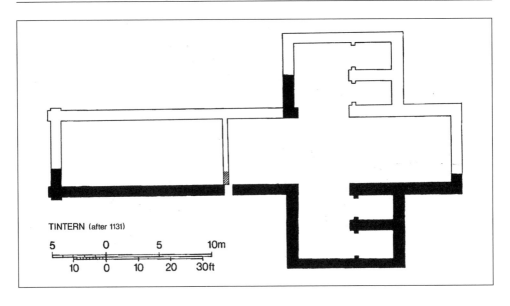

TINTERN (after 1131)

11   *The first church at Tintern (after Brakspear).*

Harold Brakspear and William Hope. Because the site was liable to flooding, floor levels had been raised substantially, and these early buildings had been buried to a depth of 1.5-2m, ensuring their survival . The church was a remarkably plain building with a short, square presbytery, shallow transepts with a single eastern chapel, and a long, aisleless nave, built of finely cut stone and with the simplest architectural detailing. Unfortunately, only small parts of it were examined and its internal layout was not recovered. It must have been built in the early 1130s, making it the earliest known Cistercian church. The cloister, some 29.3m square, lay on the south side of the church, and followed what has been called the 'undeveloped' Cistercian layout. Slightly later than the church, its buildings too were of carefully cut stone, and internal wall-faces were covered with thick plaster which was painted white. The cloister ranges were modest in scale, only 8.2m wide internally, a measurement used widely for early domestic buildings within the order. The east range butted against the south transept of the church and was only of a single storey, for unlike most Cistercian houses, the dormitory was on the ground floor at the southern end of the range. At the north end was the chapter house where the business of the monastery was conducted, faults confessed, and penances given, contained within the range, and between it and the dormitory was the parlour where talking was permitted in the cloister at strictly limited times. The south range comprised the refectory, laid out parallel to the south cloister alley in the Benedictine fashion, and the kitchen, rooms Brakspear failed to find, though he found the sites of their doors from the cloister. The west range, which housed the lay brothers, was of two storeys, with cellarage and their refectory on the ground floor and their dormitory above. A drain taken off the River Wey flushed latrines attached to both dormitories.

Thus, by about 1135, Waverley had a permanent cloister layout and a permanent church. The small scale of these buildings reflected the second or missionary phase of the abbey's development, for as new recruits joined the community experienced monks were dispatched to establish daughter houses. From these buildings, groups were sent out to colonise the abbeys of Garendon in Leicestershire in 1133, Ford in Dorset in 1135, Thame in Oxfordshire in 1138, Bruern in Oxfordshire in 1147, and Combe in Warwickshire in 1150. It was only after this missionary phase was completed that the cloister buildings began to be enlarged as the number of monks and lay brothers in the house grew to 70 and 120 respectively in the 1180s.

At Tintern, a very similar plan was adopted shortly after its foundation in 1131. As at Waverley, the founding community came from L'Aumône in Normandy and some form of familial similarity should be expected. Built in the early 1130s, the church at Tintern was again a simple building (**11**), with a short square presbytery, transepts with two square eastern chapels, and an unaisled nave. Here, though, a stone screen divided the monks' choir in the eastern bays of the nave from the lay brothers' church which occupied the remainder. The cloister was on the north side of the church to take advantage of drainage from the River Wye and was 23m square. Parts of the east and north ranges survive or have been recovered by excavation, following a similar plan to that at Waverley. Here, the monks' dormitory was on the first floor, over a chapter house, parlour, day-stair, and dayroom where the monks could work within the confines of the cloister. The north range contained the refectory on an east-west alignment, with the kitchen at its west end. The original west range has not been traced. As at Waverley, the cloister ranges were 8.2m wide. Enlargement of the cloister buildings did not begin until the late twelfth century, again showing that numbers had been kept down by the founding of daughter houses; at Kingswood in Gloucestershire in 1139, and at Tintern Minor in County Wexford as late as 1190.

At Rievaulx, recent research has shown that parts of the west and east ranges belong to the first stone abbey buildings raised by Abbot William in the mid-to-late 1130s. Geophysical prospecting has located the foundations of an early church on the north side of the cloister (**12**) which is probably earlier than the building of Abbot William's permanent domestic ranges and belongs to the foundation period. Here, the northern part of a narrow west range, 8.2m wide, survives in part almost to full height, and the northern half of a contemporary east range has been traced below the later chapter house and parlour, indicating a cloister 42.5m square. The west range comprised the outer parlour, cellarage, a broad passage through the range and the lay brothers' refectory at ground floor, with their dormitory above (**col. pl. 4**). Its missing south end must have been carried on an undercroft because of the fall of the land. Subsequent remodelling makes it difficult to identify the original form of these buildings, which had virtually no architectural detailing. At Rievaulx' daughter house of Melrose, founded in 1136

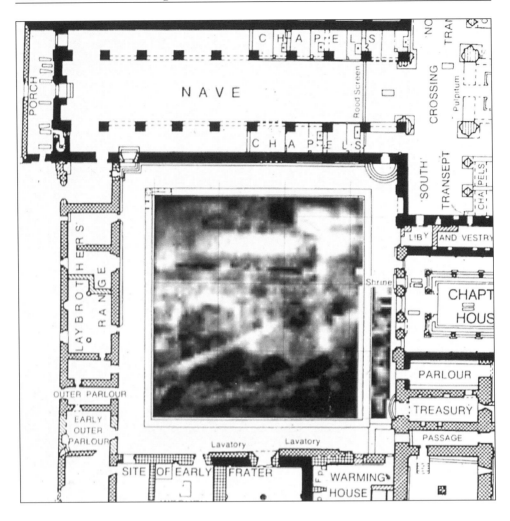

12   *The first stone church at Rievaulx, revealed by geophysical survey below the later cloister (John Syzmanski).*

and probably raising its first stone buildings in the early 1140s, fragments of the first cloister layout survive within a rebuilding of the later twelfth century. Here, the cloister lay on the north side of the church, and fragments of the refectory and lay brothers ranges survive, again buildings 8.2m wide internally. The refectory and kitchen were arranged in the Benedictine manner as at Waverley, but here an enclosed space was provided between the west range and the cloister, a lane that provided access to the outer court to the north and the church to the south for the lay brothers, keeping them quite separate from the choir monks. There was almost certainly a similar feature at Rievaulx, though it has not been traced.

It is to Fountains we must turn to see an almost complete set of cloister buildings, raised by Abbot Henry Murdac between 1144 when he became abbot,

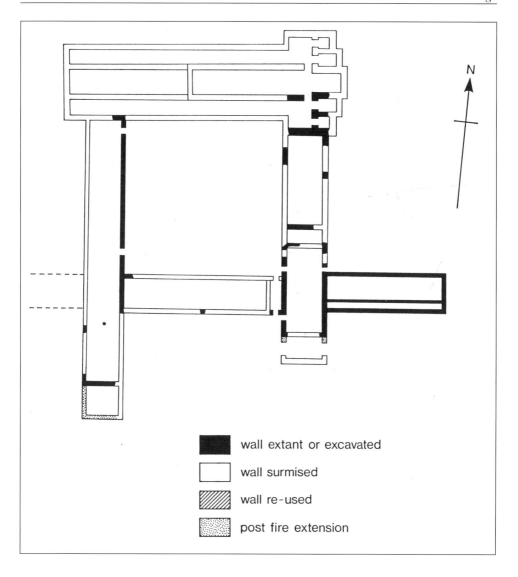

N

13   *The ground plan of Fountains in 1146 at the time the abbey was damaged by fire. Parts of the east
      and west ranges still stand to full height.*

and 1146 when they were burned out (**13**). Clairvaux-trained and the builder of
the first permanent buildings at Vauclair on the River Somme, his buildings
would therefore represent the latest in Cistercian architectural philosophy. When
he first arrived in Yorkshire he must have been appalled by what he found; a small
church and timber domestic buildings from which colonies had already been
dispatched to found daughter houses at Haverholme in 1137, at Newminster in
1138, and at Kirkstead in 1139. Substantial parts of his east, south, and west ranges

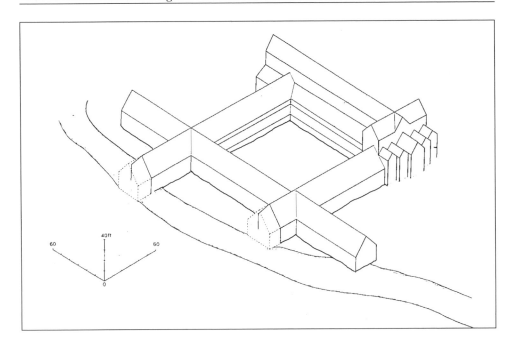

14   A schematic reconstruction of Fountains Abbey in 1146. Those areas shown in broken line were built when the abbey was restored after the fire.

survive to full height of 6.1m, built of roughly squared masonry which was plastered on both inside and outside faces and painted white. There is hardly any architectural detail, doors and windows were simply chamfered, and building must have been rapid, for both the east and west ranges have produced clear evidence to show they were burned out in the fire of 1146. He also added an aisled nave onto the earlier church to close the north side of the 38m square cloister his new ranges contained (**14**).

The east range, again 8.2m wide, contained the chapter house, immediately to the south of the church, a small parlour, the day stair from the cloister to the dormitory, and the monks' day room, with the dormitory above providing sufficient space for approximately 80 monks. The dormitory was lit by small round-headed windows, several of which remain. A latrine block was provided against the east wall, with a door leading from the dormitory, large enough to accommodate 40 monks at a sitting. Further latrines were placed in the south wall of this building at ground level to serve a yard that must have been entered from the day room. The south range contained an east-west aligned refectory open to the roof, with the kitchen to its west. To its east, a narrow passage ran through the range at ground floor level, and above this at the level of the dormitory was a small chamber probably occupied by the abbot who was required to sleep in the dormitory. The west range, the home of the lay brothers, was much longer than the east range, its first floor the lay brothers' dormitory 64m long and 8.2m wide, large enough to house 140 of the brethren. Their refectory occupied the southern half of the ground floor of the range and shared the monks' kitchen. At the north end of the range was the outer parlour where members of the community could meet the outside world, to the south of this cellarage, and between that and the refectory a passage into the cloister. The accommodation was designed for a community of medium size in Cistercian terms, with no room for expansion.

It was from these buildings that Fountains continued to establish daughter houses as the community attracted more recruits, at Woburn in 1145, at Lysa in Norway in 1146, at Kirkstall and Vaudey in 1147, and at Meaux in 1151. Conditions had become cramped by 1146, however, and when the damaged cloister buildings were repaired after the fire, both the east and west ranges were lengthened to extend the dormitories to house more monks and lay brothers.

3 The building of permanent monasteries

All Cistercian monasteries would have had a temporary phase following their foundation, where survival was not certain and endowments were insufficient to support building on a monumental scale. Some found their sites inconvenient, either lacking in water or too close to the distractions of the outside world, and moved to more suitable sites. The Fountains community that settled at Barnoldswick in Craven moved to a site on the Aire to the west of Leeds in 1152 having thoroughly upset the local populace, for instance, and their brothers who had settled at Haverholme on the edge of the Lincolnshire Fens moved to a better drained site in the Bishop of Lincoln's park on the east side of Louth. Similarly, the community that had settled at Castle Bytham moved fairly rapidly to their new site of Vaudey because they had too little water on their first site. Others, like the monks of Sawley found their sites inconvenient and uncomfortable but their patrons unwilling to let them move.

Once stability had been achieved, however, the building of permanent buildings could begin, and once again, there is a remarkable consistency in the buildings the Cistercians erected, buildings which are immediately recognisable even as ruins. Two types of monastery were to appear from the late 1150s in Britain, large monasteries like Fountains, Rievaulx, and Melrose designed to house more than 100 monks and to act as the heads of families like the French houses of Cîteaux, La Ferté, Pontigny, Morimond, and Clairvaux, and smaller daughter houses that housed 50 or so monks, such as Roche or Rufford, with buildings of smaller scale but identical plan that compare closely with their French counterparts of Fontenay, Noirlac, and Fontfroid, all daughter houses of Clairvaux. Smaller as these second-tier communities might be, they were still large when compared with those of other orders because they had to house both monks and lay brothers. Both can be identified instantly by their scale and simplicity. Their appearance in the landscape from the middle of the twelfth century was stunning. The fact that they painted their early buildings white can only have added to the effect.

The first Cistercian monastery in Britain to begin the construction of its truly permanent buildings was Rievaulx Abbey. Aelred, elected as third abbot in 1147, began the wholesale rebuilding of the abbey on a monumental scale to allow the

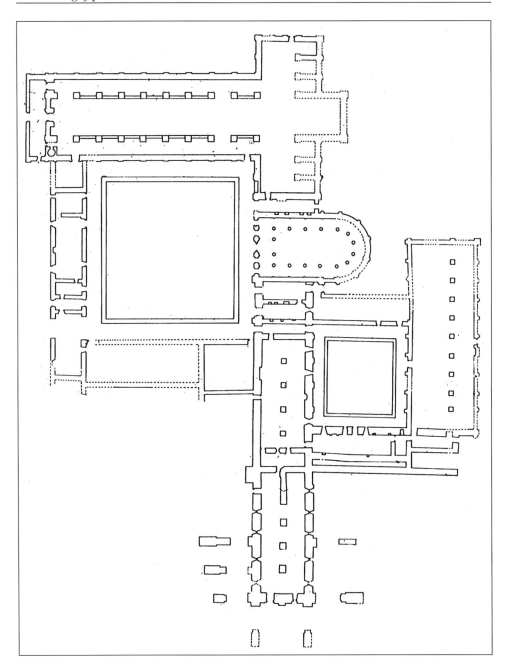

15   *Ground plan of Aelred's new monastery at Rievaulx, built between 1147 and 1160. The west range of the cloister was built slighly earlier by Abbot William, its smaller scale showing how rapidly the community was growing in the 1150s.*

community to grow (**15**). Rievaulx had established five daughter houses, at Warden and Melrose in 1136, at Dundrennan in 1142, at Revesby in 1143, and at Rufford in 1146, and when Aelred became abbot in the following year he took the decision to consolidate the community, letting the number of monks rise to 150 and the number of lay brothers and servants to some 500. Fountains Abbey established its last daughter house in 1151, and then began a similar pattern of rebuilding as the community expanded rapidly. Melrose, intended from the start to be the centre of the Cistercian reform in Scotland, also began its great permanent buildings in the 1150s, following the establishment of daughter houses at Newbattle in 1140 and Kinloss and Holmcultram in 1150. In each case, the growth of the community and scale of building was dependent on patronage, and it was the lack of external support which prevented the early mission centre of Waverley from rebuilding its early, undeveloped stone buildings until the end of the twelfth century.

Both Fountains and Rievaulx attracted massive support in areas of sparse population that was ideal for their highly centralised techniques of farming and had abbots who were skilful administrators capable of building efficient estates. Melrose was directly supported by the Scots King David, a close friend of Abbot Aelred of Rievaulx.

The buildings that began to appear in the 1150s were monumental, with churches that followed the design of the recently completed church at Clairvaux. Though they differed slightly in their elevations, the churches at Rievaulx, Melrose, and Fountains, were built to a common plan that can also be seen in the first stone church at Fountains: a short square-ended presbytery to house the altar, deep transepts with three eastern chapels in each where the inner chapels were extended along the sides of the presbytery, and a long aisled nave that housed both the monks' choir and that of the lay brothers (**16**). The church of Fountains' third daughter house of Newminster, being built at about the same time as the church at Rievaulx by Abbot Robert (Chapter 2) had an alternate and more typically 'Bernardine' plan, where the inner transept chapels were arranged in line, though it appears to have shared the same architectural massing as the Rievaulx church. As originally designed, none of these churches had a tower at the crossing, and their architectural embellishment was reduced to the minimum. Sufficient remains at Rievaulx to reconstruct the elevation of the 1150s nave with its chamfered square piers and pointed arches, apparently the design used also at Newminster and Margam, and probably at Whitland, while the nave at Fountains, built in the 1160s on the site of a planned unaisled nave remains intact, with cylindrical piers and a taller elevation (**17**). The two-storey elevation was typical of early Cistercian churches, and the use of pointed arches for the arcades which were carried back to the aisle walls as transverse barrel vaults was a feature derived from the order's Burgundian homeland. The Rievaulx church was built of rubble with cut stone used only for its detailing, and here a typically Cistercian feature can be seen. All the freestone detail is cut to a standard series of templates and each different element has a Roman numeral cut into its face. So standardised is the

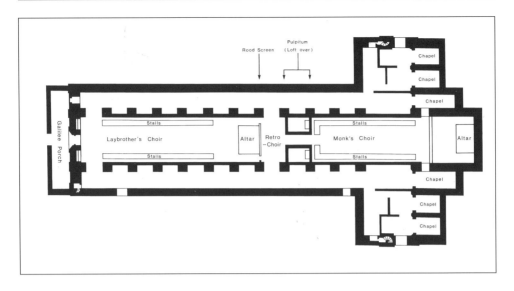

16   *The new church at Fountains, begun in the early 1150s, was effectively two churches divided by the rood screen with the lay brothers in the nave and the monks occupying the eastern half. Its barn-like interior was never meant to be seen as one volume but as a series of discrete spaces (after Fergusson with corrections and additions).*

construction that the building was designed in kit-form for rapid erection by semi-skilled labour. The Fountains church, however, is built entirely of ashlar, and being some 10 to 20 years later in its construction, has an increasing number of decorative elements. Both buildings, however, were plastered internally and externally, their walls white-limed, and a regular pattern of freestone blocks outlined in white paint.

A large part of the cloister buildings and the infirmary built before Aelred's death in 1167 survives at Rievaulx, the most complete example of a mid-twelfth-century Cistercian layout that still exists (**18**; **col. pl. 5-6**). The plan adopted was that of Henry Murdac's monastery at Fountains (**13**) with a number of innovations and a vastly increased scale. The layout was still the modified Benedictine layout first seen in Abbot Henry's 1140s cloister at Fountains, with the day stair to the dormitory in the east range and an east-west refectory. However, it was slowly starting to evolve into a mature Cistercian plan, adapted across Britain by the early 1170s. Aelred's buildings required the construction of a series of massive terraces on the side of the valley in which the original monastery was placed, a certain sign of the Cistercian single-mindedness that elsewhere moved rivers and whole populations to site their monasteries as ideally as possible. The original site at Rievaulx had been severely constrained by the narrowness of the valley floor, though it had been quite suitable for a small community. Rather than abandon it for a better site, the site itself was modified,

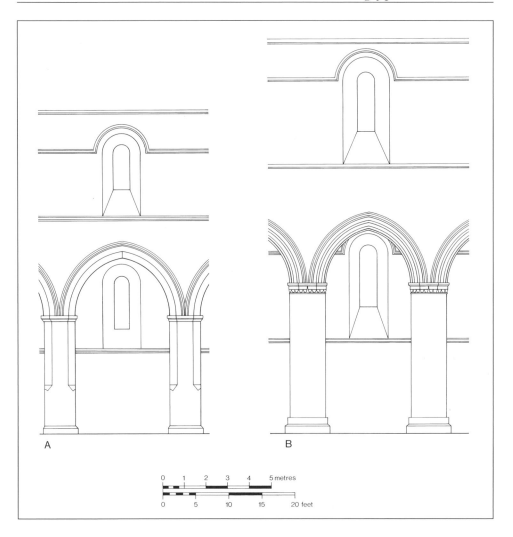

17   *Comparative elevations of the nave at Rievaulx (a) and Fountains (b) that show how rapidly Cistercian church design was developing (after Harrison and Reeve).*

the River Rye moved from the centre of the valley by agreement with the Savigniac monks of Old Byland whose common boundary it was, and vast buildings were quickly built. All that survived of the first stone monastery was the west cloister range, which remained in part throughout the monastery's life.

Central to Aelred's new monastery was a new east range to house the growing community of monks, and containing a dormitory 75m long and 10.3m wide, supported at its north end on a vaulted undercroft which contained the parlour, the day stair to the dormitory, a passage to the infirmary, and the monks' dayroom, and at its south end on two storeys of vaulted rooms (**18**). At its centre against the

18   Aelred's great east range at Rievaulx, shortened in the late fourteenth century (author).

east wall was a vast latrine building three storeys high, with a barrel-vaulted basement, the noviciate in a fine barrel vaulted and heated room at ground floor level, with the latrines on the upper floor level with the dormitory. At Rievaulx' daughter house of Melrose, the east range and latrine block were rebuilt at about the same date to an almost identical plan. Between the church and the east range was the chapter house (**19**), a unique building in the Cistercian world, an aisled apsidal building of great beauty and distinguished by its use of decorative capitals and corbels. Its unique design springs from two sources: Aelred's desire to provide accommodation for the vast army of lay brothers who exceptionally under his rule attended chapter meetings to hear the abbot's sermon and sat on both sides of the aisle segregated from the monks; and to provide a fitting setting for the burial of the sanctified first abbot, William. Aelred chose the form of the Roman martyrium church, expressed in the best mid-twelfth-century Cistercian architecture. Aelred also rebuilt the south range of the cloister, to contain an east-west refectory with a kitchen to the west, set over an undercroft which still survives in part filled up to the level of the cloister in a later rebuilding.

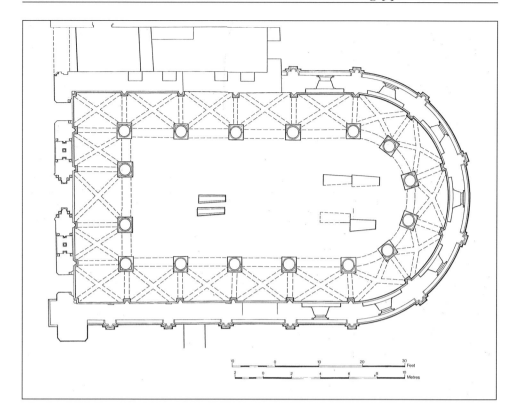

19   *The apsidal chapter house at Rievaulx, built by Aelred to house the grave of the first abbot, William, in the 1150s. Its design reflects his own ideas of Cistercian brotherhood with seating for the lay brothers in the aisles (after Harrison).*

His most important building, however, was the infirmary (**20**), erected in the late 1150s at the east end of the monks' latrine block, separated from the east range by a second cloister. It is the oldest surviving Cistercian infirmary building, a great hall of 10 bays with an aisle on its east side in which the beds were placed. At its south-east corner was a chapel and at its south end a latrine and bath-house. Although it was substantially altered in about 1500, sufficient remains to be certain about its original form.

The contribution of the Savigniac monasteries

In 1147, the abbot of Savigny in Normandy, an abbey with 10 daughter houses and three grand daughters in England and Wales, was converted to the Cistercian reform by Abbot Bernard of Clairvaux, bringing all his abbey's dependencies,

20   The infirmary hall at Rievaulx, the oldest surviving Cistercian infirmary (author)

whether they liked it or not, into the Cistercian fold. The oldest and greatest of these monasteries was Furness, founded by Count Stephen of Boulogne (later King Stephen) at Tulketh near Preston in 1123 but moved to the Furness peninsular in 1127. Savigny's other daughters were Basingwerk, Buckfast, Buildwas, Byland, Coggeshall, Combermere, Neath, Quarr, and Stratford Langthorne, all founded between 1131 and 1140, and Furness had three daughter houses at Calder and Swineshead, both established in 1135, and Rushen founded in 1138. In theory at least, they all became Cistercian on 17 September 1147. The process, even where it took place without dissent, required retraining for the monks, the process being graphically revealed at Swineshead where Abbot Aelred of Revesby (and later Rievaulx) was sent to 'illuminate it with Cistercian way of life' and where a new abbot, Gilbert de Hoyland, a monk of Clairvaux, was imposed in 1148 by St Bernard. The architecture of the Savigniacs differed from that of the Cistercians, to the extent that their churches at least had to be substantially rebuilt. Furness, perhaps fearful of losing its status, originally refused to join the Cistercians but was finally coerced.

At Buildwas, it would appear that the Savigniacs had not progressed far with their church, and what began building in about 1150 was a small church roughly contemporary with the new church at Fountains (**col. pl. 7**), typical of British churches of the mid-twelfth century. With a two-storey elevation, transepts with

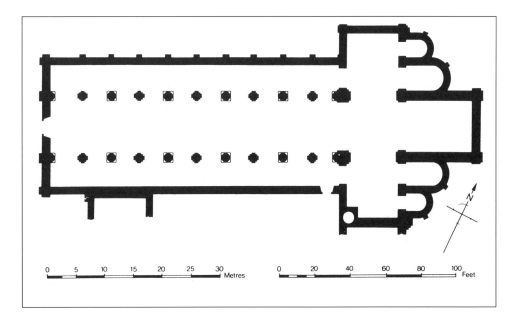

21   *The Savigniac church at Furness, which survives in part, differed from the plan form adopted by the
      Cistercians and was substantially rebuilt when the community joined the reform (after Hope and
      Dickinson).*

two square eastern chapels, and a small square-ended presbytery, it was designed
originally without a tower at the crossing. As at Fountains, a tower was added in
the course of building, probably after 1157 when the General Chapter of the order
amended their statutes to the effect that 'stone towers with bells be not built'. As
the Buildwas tower was not a belfry but a lantern to light the choir below, it was
therefore permissible. Previously, towers were not permitted.

Excavation and a detailed examination of what survives of the twelfth century
church at Furness has revealed the sea-change the Savigniacs underwent as they
became Cistercians (**21**). The first church at Furness, begun in the early 1130s
followed the Benedictine plan with an apsed presbytery and apsidal transept
chapels arranged *en echelon*, with an aisled nave of 10 bays. Of this, the crossing
piers, part of the south transept, and the south wall of the nave survive. Most of
the nave had not been raised before 1147 though the eastern parts of the church
were probably complete. It was convertible to Cistercian form by rebuilding the
transepts and presbytery, and completing the nave. The crossing was raised in
height, which implies that the height of the nave was raised from that which was
originally planned. The reason for this lay in the elevation of the new transepts
which included a triforium or gallery storey between the eastern arcade and the
clerestorey windows. Built in the 1160s, and thus a decade later than the new
church at Fountains, this is the earliest incidence in Britain of the Cistercians

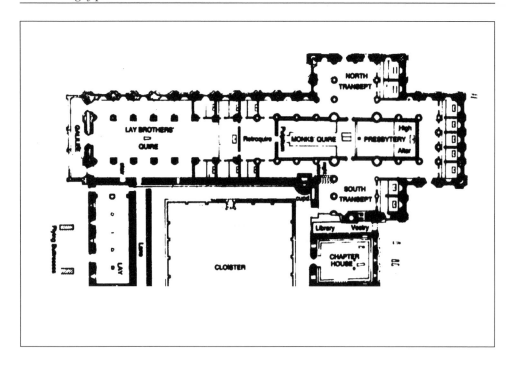

22   *The great church at Byland was the first Cistercian church to depart from the standard Bernardine plan
in Britain and one of the largest to be built by the order. In contrast, the cloister ranges are small and
austere.*

adopting a three-storey elevation, a softening of their approach to architecture.
The nave, built in the 1170s, had alternating circular and clustered piers and a
three-storey elevation, a building that marked the transition from Romanesque to
Gothic.

More remarkable was the new monastery that rose at Byland from the 1160s.
Built on a reclaimed marsh which required the drainage of a broad valley, it had
the first Cistercian church in Britain to depart from the standard plans first seen
at Rievaulx and Newminster (**22**). This was not the first church to be planned at
the site, but incorporated the remains of an earlier and slightly smaller church that
was probably 'Bernardine' in form. Begun in the 1170s and not completed until
the early thirteenth century, the church at Byland was aisled throughout, with
chapels on both the east and west sides of the transepts, a feature of the great
church at Clairvaux, and a presbytery of three bays with an aisle against its east
wall that contained five chapels, a feature seen by 1193 at Cîteaux and Morimond.
It was a very different church from any others of its date in Britain, and it marked
the next stage in the development of Cistercian architecture. It was light and
spacious, with fine but restrained architectural detailing, and a three-storey

elevation (**col. pl. 8**) that was more developed than that at Furness. Unlike the earlier churches of the order, it was not borrowing French designs but was purely English in its inspiration. From the 1170s there were two models from which other Cistercian churches could take their inspiration.

The building of smaller monasteries

Some Cistercian monasteries were never intended to become as large as the mother houses of the order, but remained modest in scale, their buildings scaled down versions of the great houses. They were intended for no more than 50 monks and perhaps 100 lay brethren, and comprise the bulk of the order's houses in Britain. Buildwas falls into this class and is perhaps the best example to survive (**23**). Built between 1150 and 1170 and thus contemporary with both Rievaulx and Fountains, it shows the economies of scale found in a second tier house. The church, barely altered since it was built, is small but contains exactly the same elements as its larger contemporaries. The restrained decoration is the same, and the same two storey elevation with pointed arcades and round-headed windows is maintained. The monks' choir occupied the crossing and eastern bay of the nave, and the lay brothers occupied the western half of the nave in the usual way, their stalls placed against low walls between the piers, the scars of which remain.

However, the significance of this church is that unlike its larger contemporaries it was never rebuilt or enlarged. It was designed for a small community which was not expected to grow, and which had limited financial resources. Daughter houses were never well endowed, and Buildwas was no exception, its estates being restricted to Shropshire and the Welsh borderland. If Fountains had a cloister 38m square, Buildwas had a cloister of only 25m, placed to the north of the church to take advantage of drainage from the River Severn. Its cloister ranges were only 8.2m wide, identical to the pre-expansion or mission stage buildings in the great houses. The provision was exactly the same, however. The east range (**24**) contained the library and sacristy against the church, an exquisite chapter house and parlour, and the day room which had an open arcade on its east side to provide access to an open yard which later became the infirmary cloister. The dormitory, only 34m long, occupied the whole of the upper floor, and would have housed a maximum of 40 monks. Their refectory, in the north range, lay east-west in the early Cistercian manner, with the day stair to its east and kitchen to the west. The west range housed the lay brothers, its southern end raised on a basement. Its precise layout can no longer be determined, though it was separated from the monks' cloister by a walled lane, a feature peculiar to the Cistercians but never used consistently in their planning.

Contemporary with the church at Buildwas was the church built in the 1150s at Sawley (**6, 46**) and probably not much later than the church of its mother house of Newminster. Only the presbytery, transepts, and first bay of the nave were built initially, and the ground plan of the eastern end is that of Newminster. The thick

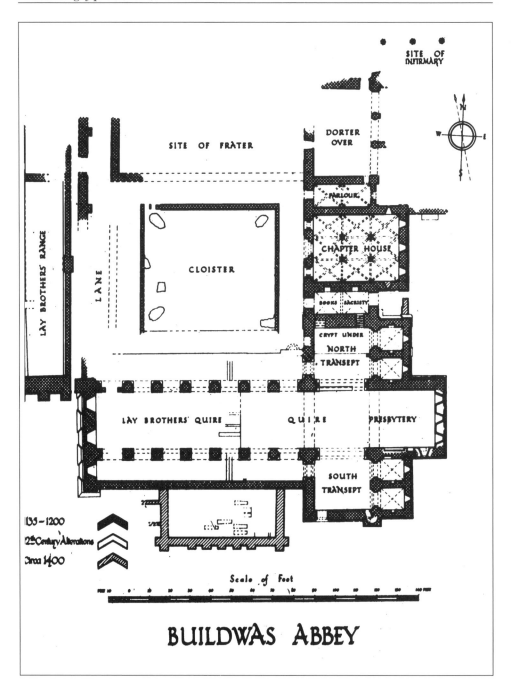

23   *The ground plan of Buildwas is typical of many smaller Cistercian monasteries, never intended to*
      house a large community but sharing the same general layout as the greater houses of the order.

24   The east range of the cloister at Buildwas remains substantially complete (author).

walls of the presbytery suggest that it was covered by a barrel vault like its contemporary sister house of Kirkstall originally had. The elevation of the transepts is, however, that of Fountains and probably derives from Vauclair. It predates Fountains slightly, however, and suggests that the design was being tried out in a smaller member of the family before the mother house committed itself. More remarkable is the nave, which was designed from the first to be unaisled. When the church was completed in the 1170s, no attempt was made to add aisles to the nave, and the form was obviously deliberate. It is not unique, for excavation has shown that the 1150s church at Fountains was designed with an unaisled nave of which it seems the first five bays were probably built.

Slightly later than Buildwas and Sawley are two small houses that show the development of the Cistercian plan to maturity. Rufford, founded in Sherwood Forest in 1146, was the last daughter house of Rievaulx; and Roche founded in the following year from Newminster was a grand daughter house of Fountains. Close neighbours, they demonstrate a consistency that shows that architectural development was still closely and centrally controlled in the second half of the twelfth century, and they are typical of all Cistercian daughter houses raised in the third quarter of the twelfth century.

Rufford was a poor house, never able to build up close estates because of its location in the royal forest of Sherwood. Its plan (**25**) is only known from excavation apart from the west range which was retained as part of a post-Suppression house.

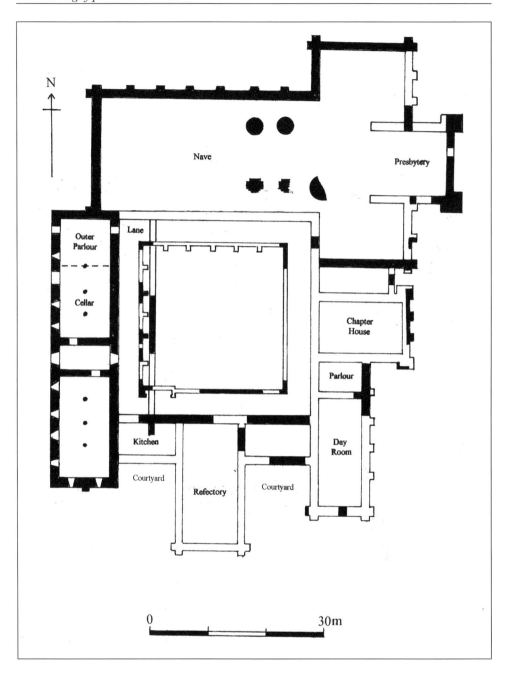

N

Nave

Presbytery

Outer
Parlour

Lane

Cellar

Chapter
House

Parlour

Kitchen

Day
Room

Courtyard

Refectory

Courtyard

0   30m

25   *The plan of Rufford Abbey, largely demolished when it was converted to a house in the sixteenth century has been recovered by excavation and geophysical survey (after McGee).*

It is clear that building was fairly slow, work beginning in the church in the late 1150s, but the south and west ranges of the cloister not being completed until the 1170s or 80s. It is particularly significant for one reason. The lay brothers' accommodation in the west range was separated from the cloister by a lane as at Buildwas and Kirkstall in the 1160s, and at Sawley (**7**) as late as the 1190s. Where a lane occurred, a separate cloister was never provided for the lay brothers. Where there was no lane, a cloister was provided, as at Fountains, to the west of the west range. In such a centralised order there appears to be no consistency, or at least two separate models in providing for the lay brethren.

At Roche (**col. pl. 8**), permanent buildings were not provided before the 1170s but once begun were completed rapidly within a decade and extended a few years later, allowing a snapshot of Cistercian development at its most mature. The church was built with a three-storey elevation and vaulted throughout, a design that was becoming gothic and remarkably French in inspiration, probably brought from Vauclair near Laon. The connection was Abbot Richard III of Fountains, who was head of the family that contained Roche and who had previously been abbot of Vauclair. Although the elevation was revolutionary in a small daughter house, the plan of the church was little changed from that of Buildwas or Fountains. The abbeys of Dundrennan (**col. pl. 10**), the eastern parts of whose church were remodelled in the 1180s, and Kirkstead and Holmcultram, built perhaps a few years earlier, share the same detailing, suggesting that there was a consistency in the churches built in the 1170s and 80s that matched those of the previous generation. It was in the planning of the cloister buildings that the greatest change can be seen. Gone is the old Benedictine layout, replaced by a plan which is typically Cistercian, developed ultimately from the rebuilt Clairvaux.

The south range of the cloister, with a central refectory placed at a right-angle to the cloister alley between the warming house and the kitchen was an innovation which first appeared in Britain in the late 1160s at Kirkstall. Indeed, the south range at Kirkstall was being built at about the time the change in layout became fashionable here, and the layout of the refectory was changed from an east-west to a north-south alignment in the course of building. Roche followed her grandmother Fountains, where a new refectory was begun in about 1170 (**26**), the first truly gothic building to appear there. The purpose of rotating the refectory through 90 degrees has long been debated, but the reason is probably one of simple practicality. It permitted the inclusion of both the warming house with its fire-places and the kitchen in the south range, freeing up the ground floor of the east range for manual labour which was central to Cistercian life, and bringing the kitchen, shared by the monks' and lay brothers' refectories more closely into the enclosure of the cloister. Cistercian monks were not permitted to leave the cloister, and the earlier design had left them little space.

By the 1180s, two types of Cistercian monastery had appeared in Britain typified by the planning of their churches, the 'Bernardine' type which was derived from the church at Clairvaux built in Bernard's lifetime, and a more developed type which developed from the church of Byland, and which was

26   *The 1170's refectory at Fountains was originally divided by a central arcade which supported a double pitched roof, replaced by a single span in the fifteenth century. Although the wall pulpit has gone, the footpaces and the stumps of the stone table legs remain (English Heritage).*

paralleled by new churches raised at Cîteaux and Morimond at about the same time. Both were distinctly Cistercian in their conception and their spread was familial for the most part. There were exceptions, however. At Meaux, where the abbey church was taken down in the 1160s because it was thought to be unsuitable, the new church which rose in its place did not have the 'Bernardine' plan of the new church which was almost complete at the mother house of Fountains, but had an aisled presbytery that followed the example of Byland, suggesting that either plan was acceptable within the best regulated of families. The cloister plan, however, was much more certain, and was that of Fountains, Sawley, and Roche; all of them following the layout first established at Clairvaux in the 1140s but not reaching Britain until the 1160s.

Cistercian nuns

The effect of the appearance of the Cistercians in Britain was dramatic, partly because of their religious fervour and partly because they caught the spirit of the time. They had brought a new vitality and a new architecture to religious life. Not only did they appeal to men, but also to women who made up a significant proportion of the religious world. Houses of Benedictine and Cluniac nuns had begun to appear in some numbers since the beginning of the twelfth century, and it was not long before moves were made to introduce the reform to women. Gilbert, the rector of Sempringham in Lincolnshire, gathered a group of nuns in the 1130s who he hoped to bring within the Cistercian rule. The order would have nothing to do with them. Indeed, women were totally excluded from Cistercian monasteries and their granges, and Bernard of Clairvaux in particular had to advise Gilbert that his nuns could not be accepted, leaving him to establish his own order that combined women living under a form of the Cistercian rule in double monasteries where their spiritual needs were served by canons following the rule of St Augustine. The Gilbertines provided one outlet for religious women who wanted to follow the reform, but this was by no means the only one. Before 1150 no fewer than eight nunneries had been established for women who claimed to be 'Cistercian', all of them in Yorkshire and Lincolnshire, areas strongly influenced by Fountains and Rievaulx and by the Gilbertines. On what basis they claimed this distinction is uncertain, and three of them, Swine, Heynings, and Stixwould were originally double houses like the Gilbertine monasteries that were starting to appear in the same area. The nunneries of Gokewell, Greenfield, Handale, Kirklees, and Nun Cotham were simply nunneries whose inmates followed the Cistercian reform and wore the white habit without the complication of canons following other rules resident. Little is known of their buildings or their economy, for unlike the White Monks they were poorly endowed and their buildings small and often insubstantial. None of these has any standing remains, though Gokewell survives as a fine earthwork site, a rectangular precinct little more than 5 acres (2ha) in extent.

The site of Kirklees was excavated in the early part of this century (**27**), providing a fairly reliable plan of the church and cloister which can be checked against a description made in 1535. It is a fairly typical nunnery plan, which probably reflects the twelfth century form of the house, at least in outline, but there is nothing 'Cistercian' about it. The church is a plain rectangle on the north side of the tiny cloister, and the cloister ranges themselves reflect the size and relative poverty of the community. In planning its is neither the Benedictine layout of the early twelfth-century Cistercian monks, or the developed Cistercian plan that was appearing in the 1160s in Britain. It is, in fact, the plan adopted by the Augustinian canons from the early twelfth century, with an east-west refectory at first floor level in the south range. Their buildings which provide the very framework of monastic life do not immediately identify the nuns as Cistercians. Only at Swine, a somewhat wealthier house, do we have any evidence for a

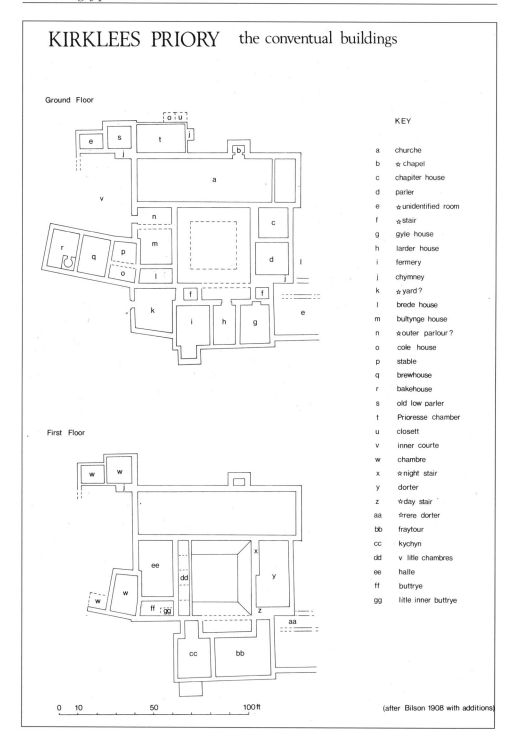

KIRKLEES PRIORY the conventual buildings

Ground Floor

KEY

a   churche
b   ☆ chapel
c   chapiter house
d   parler
e   ☆unidentified room
f   ☆stair
g   gyle house
h   larder house
i   fermery
j   chymney
k   ☆ yard ?
l   brede house
m   bultynge house
n   ☆outer parlour ?
o   cole house
p   stable
q   brewhouse
r   bakehouse
s   old low parler
t   Prioresse chamber
u   closett
v   inner courte
w   chambre
x   ☆night stair
y   dorter
z   ☆day stair
aa ☆rere dorter
bb fraytour
cc kychyn
dd v litle chambres
ee halle
ff buttrye
gg litle inner buttrye

First Floor

0   10   50   100 ft

(after Bilson 1908 with additions)

27   *Reconstructed plan of the Cistercian nunnery of Kirkless, based on the evidence of a sixteenth-century survey and excavations carried out in 1904-05.*

28   The nuns' church at Swine, drawn in 1784 before the crossing tower and stubs of the transepts were demolished (from Poulson 1840). Though the eastern arm was rebuilt in the fourteenth century, the western crossing arch shows that there was a cruciform church here in the second half of the twelfth century.

cruciform church (**28**). Here, the crossing, demolished in the 1780s, dated from the middle years of the twelfth century, and shows clear evidence of an unaisled nave and eastern transept chapels. The presbytery was rebuilt in the fourteenth century, removing any evidence of its original form. Because there were originally canons and lay brothers as well as nuns and lay sisters here, it is uncertain whether the eastern parts of the church or the unaisled nave was originally the nuns' church. Alternatively, the architectural form of the church might have been copying the greater Cistercian churches. We simply do not know.

The general picture, confirmed by the scant remains of late twelfth-century 'Cistercian' nunneries is that the nuns chose, or had imposed upon them, the simplest form of monastic life which was consistent with the reformed rule of St Benedict, but that they lacked the central control of Cistercian legislation and were not organised formally into families. The only true Cistercian features they seem to have is that they chose sites which were well removed from the outside world and they chose the white habit of reform. Occasionally, they recolonised an earlier religious site as at Llanllyr as the monks of Melrose had done, but their sites were normally chosen for solitude alone. They provided at best a form of the Cistercian reform that differenced them from other nuns, but this did not make them the female equivalent of Cistercian monks.

4 The development of abbeys from the late twelfth century

By the 1170s, the White Monks had almost completed their colonisation of Britain, with substantial families of monasteries firmly settled in almost every part of the country. Indeed, the General Chapter of the order decreed in 1152 that no new daughter houses were to be established; the time had come to consolidate, to complete permanent buildings, to rationalise estates, and to concentrate on religious life. Although this was largely observed in England, colonisation was to continue in Scotland and Wales for some time.

The 1160s and 70s were a remarkable period of building for the Cistercians. Twenty or more years of settlement had brought stability, populations had begun to rise, and a second generation of monks had matured, monks who had not known the hardships of the first settlers but who sought the same spiritual purity. Wealth brought the ability to build for the future, and the move towards gothic buildings which had begun to emerge in the 1160s took hold in the buildings that began to arise in the last two decades of the twelfth century.

Romanesque architecture, heavy and dark, with great piers and small round-headed windows had marked the first permanent buildings of the White Monks in Britain. Its solidity and simplicity commended itself to the early Cistercians, though they themselves were architectural innovators. They were among the first to take up new ideas in architecture. Perhaps the first was Robert of Pipewell, abbot of Fountains, who completed the cloister buildings there (**29**) in the 1170s, raising what the chronicler of the abbey described thirty years later as 'sumptuous buildings'. The main building was a new refectory (**col. pl. 11**) a few years later than that at Roche, a remarkable building with tall windows filled with grisaille glass and a central arcade that supported the roof. In contrast to the slightly earlier refectories of Kirkstall and Byland, it was a remarkably light building, very restrained in its decoration but dramatic in its effect. At Byland, plain and utilitarian cloister ranges had accompanied a startling church; at Fountains, any pretence of utility had finally been abandoned.

It was not just in the great abbeys that this happened. At Sawtry, a grand daughter of Rievaulx in the fens of Cambridgeshire, an identical design, albeit on a smaller scale, was used for the refectory at the close of the twelfth century. Some ten years after the Fountains building, the refectory at Rievaulx itself was rebuilt by Abbot Sylvan. Set on an undercroft to raise it to the level of the cloister itself the new refectory took the design used at Fountains and improved it (**30**). Gone was the central arcade, opening up the whole of the room, and the whole was

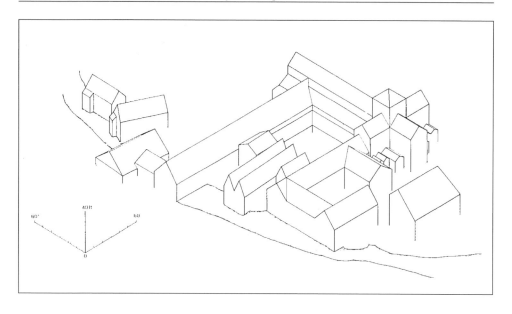

29   By 1180, the permanent cloister ranges and church at Fountains had been completed, the west and south
      ranges being built in the new gothic style, its earliest use in a British Cistercian monastery.

30   The refectory at Rievaulx, raised over a basement because of falling ground. Though it has lost its
      floor and roof, it remains a remarkably elegant building with fine, if restrained detailing (author).

31   The eastern arm and transepts of the church at Abbey Dore, re-roofed and given a tower in the seventeenth century when it became the parish church, provides the finest example to survive of an aisled presbytery with an ambulatory and eastern chapels set in an aisle against the east wall (James).

unified by linking the windows with a continuous wall arcade. What is particularly significant is that this building replaced Abbot Aelred's refectory which was only 30 years old. The new north-south alignment had become an imperative, and the status of the refectory had risen to match that of church and chapter house. If the inspiration was continental, and the refectory at Fountains is little more than a development of the refectory at Fonteney and probably Vauclair, the design is purely English. It is hardly surprising that the reform would adapt local designs, particularly when the abbots of British houses were now trained within British families. Once it was thought that such rich buildings showed a decline in Cistercian orthodoxy, where wealth had overcome simplicity. Today, it is seen as a natural development, marking subtle changes in religious life. The new buildings, still painted inside and out, were suffused with light, and it comes as no surprise to learn that the Cistercians saw light as the personification of the Holy Spirit.

In the last years of the twelfth century, Cistercian liturgy was changing, and the old, dark, and restricted presbyteries of even the great Bernardine churches were too cramped to permit the more elaborate services which were developing. In particular, the number of monks who were ordained priests had risen and they required altar space to say private masses. Additionally, success in seeking patronage brought an obligation for prayers and petitions for the laity who supported the White Monks. In time, patrons would even be buried within the

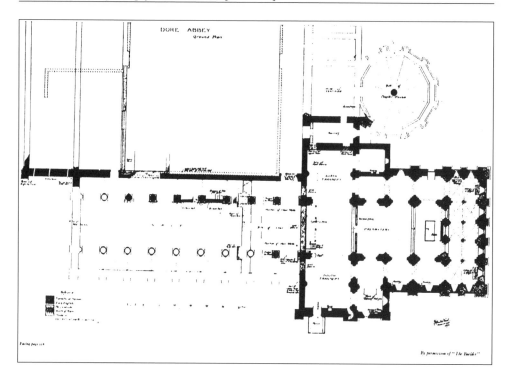

*32   Roland Paul's plan of the church and chapter house at Abbey Dore (*The Builder *1895).*

church, though in the late twelfth century they had to make do with the galilee porch at the west end of the nave. The building of the great church at Byland provided one model for the development of Cistercian churches, and from the 1190s the White Monks were to experiment with different types of churches as their reform continued to develop.

Begun about 1200, the eastern arm of Abbey Dore, founded in 1147 as a daughter house of Morimond, was replaced by a new aisled presbytery with an eastern ambulatory (**31**), vaulted throughout, and remarkably light in its architectural treatment. What is surprising is that the presbytery it replaced was less than thirty years old, suggesting that it was a response to major liturgical changes. At Dore, it was not the only change afoot. Slightly earlier than the extension of the church was the rebuilding of the chapter house, replacing a simple room contained within the east range with a ten-sided room to the east, with the old room being converted to a vestibule (**32**). This was not the only unusual Cistercian chapter house, for the monks of Margam replaced theirs with a circular building at about the same time, and the monks of Whalley were to build an octagonal chapter house when they began their new monastery in the early fourteenth century. The chapter house was, as well as the place where faults were confessed, punishments given, and business transacted, the burial place of the abbots, and it is tempting to see its rebuilding on a grand scale at Dore and

1 A contemporary illustration of Abbot Stephen Harding.

here·mmi
pluref inta
fancte fe in
i omif quos
ndof inne
fe omnē ho
mmumera
ecū omif au
tt· cū corba
acuf iob q́
mire dille
extolli p
ut dñi deftru-

VI
CON
TRA

VERITATIS VERBA
in allegatione deficiunt sepe eciā nota

2 *A Cistercian lay brother, tonsured like a monk but wearing a brown habit.*

3 *The timber monastery and the first stone church at Fountains.*

4   *Abbot William's west range of about 1140 at Rievaulx.*

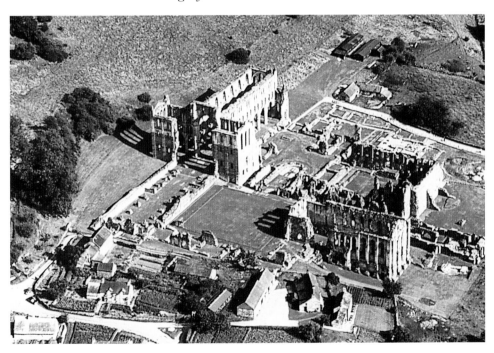

5   *Rievaulx Abbey is perhaps the most important Cistercian abbey to survive from the middle of the twelfth century.*

6   *Aelred's cloister arcade at Rievaulx.*

7   *The mid-twelfth-century church at Buildwas.*

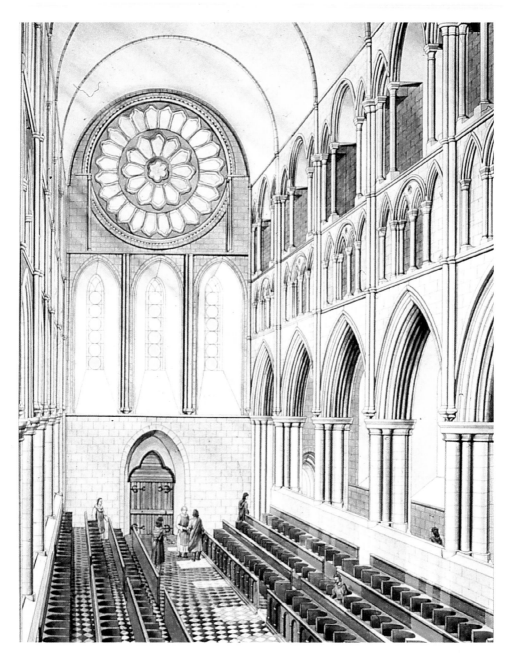

8   *The lay brothers' choir in the nave at Byland Abbey.*

9   The church at Roche.

10   The church at Dundrennan, completed in the 1180s.

11   Robert of Pipewell's south cloister range at Fountains.

12   John of York and John of Kent's new presbytery at Fountains, completed in the 1230s.

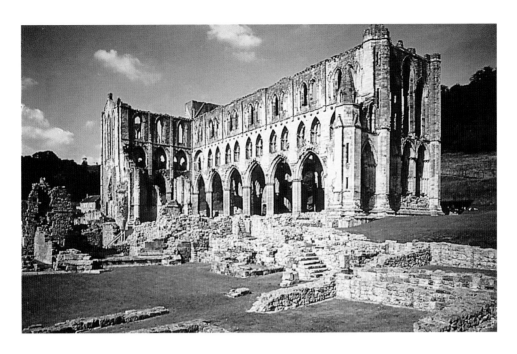

13   *The early thirteenth century presbytery and transepts at Rievaulx.*

14   *The Benedictine presbytery and transepts at Whitby.*

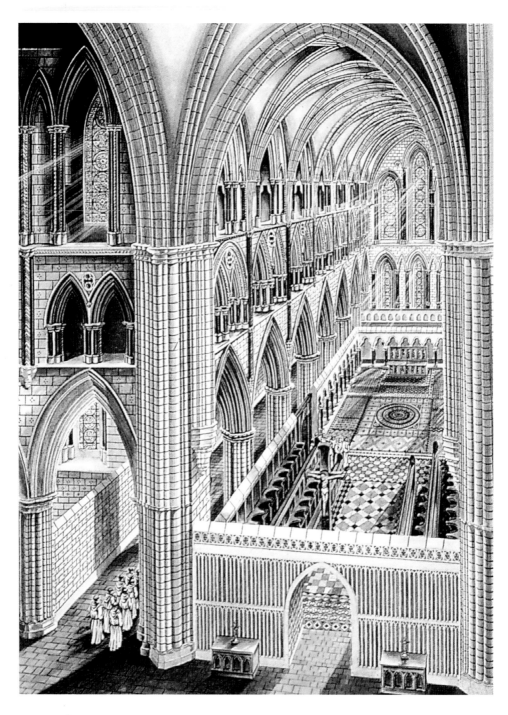

15 *The interior of the presbytery at Rievaulx.*

16   *The church at the New Abbey, looking west from the site of Devorgilla's tomb.*

17   *A reconstruction of the choir at Valle Crucis (Terry Ball for Cadw).*

18   The easternmost chapel in the north nave aisle at Rievaulx.

19   One of two early sixteenth century oak bench ends from the monks' choir at Jervaulx.

20   *Sawley Abbey, the scene of open revolt in 1536.*

21   *Abbot Dovell's great gatehouse built at Cleeve in the early sixteenth century.*

22   Evidence for the wedges that were used to cut the piers at Rievaulx.

23   *The ruins of Calder Abbey were simply left to moulder away, for they lay in an area where stone was plentiful.*

Margam as one of the emerging signs of abbatial power.

From the last years of the twelfth century the White Monks were to experience a sudden resurgence in England, the result of the patronage of King John. John was an unlikely patron, who began his relationship with the Cistercians badly. In 1200, desperately short of money, he tried to tax the Cistercians although they were normally exempt from taxation and could not pay without the consent of the General Chapter. An offer of 1000 marks (£666) was refused and John seized all livestock belonging to Cistercian houses which was pastured within the Royal Forests. Representatives of the order met the King at Lincoln to seek a compromise and John was reconciled. The king agreed to found a new abbey at Faringdon in Oxfordshire on a site which was approved by the abbot of La Ferté and settled by monks from Cîteaux in 1203. Although both King Stephen and the Empress Matilda had previously supported the Cistercians, Faringdon was the first of a series of foundations that can be directly related to the royal household, significantly raising the status of the order in England to that already enjoyed in Scotland and Wales.

Royal abbeys

The new community at Faringdon moved the following year to a new site in the New Forest that they called Beaulieu or *de bello loco* (the beautiful place) and began the construction of a permanent monastery that changed again the architectural language of the order. Only the foundations of the great church at Beaulieu survive today (**33**), begun by John but completed by his son Henry III towards the middle of the thirteenth century. In plan, the church appears to have two phases, the earliest the nine-bay nave and the south transept of what appears to be a standard late twelfth century Cistercian church, almost certainly that begun by John. The second phase comprised an apsidal presbytery containing an ambulatory with ten radiating chapels and north transept with western as well as eastern chapels and a northern porch flanked by towers. Almost certainly this represents a rebuilding by Henry III, and though similar to Clairvaux, where the presbytery had been rebuilt to house St Bernard's tomb in the 1150s, it also shares features with the presbytery of the Benedictine Westminster Abbey that Henry was rebuilding to house the shrine of Edward the Confessor. It also shares details with other French Cistercian royal foundations, the abbeys of Bonport and Royaumont, both built in the 1240s. The use of the semi-circular ambulatory appears also at Hailes, founded by Henry III's brother Richard, Earl of Cornwall in 1246, but rebuilt by his son Edmund after a fire in 1271, and at Vale Royal, begun by Edward I in 1277, and only occurs on one non-royal site, Croxden in Staffordshire, rebuilt in the early thirteenth century (**34**).

It was not only in England that royalty adopted the Cistercians. In Wales, where the first Cistercian monasteries had been planted by the English to strengthen their hold on land they had seized, it was the foundation of Strata Florida Abbey

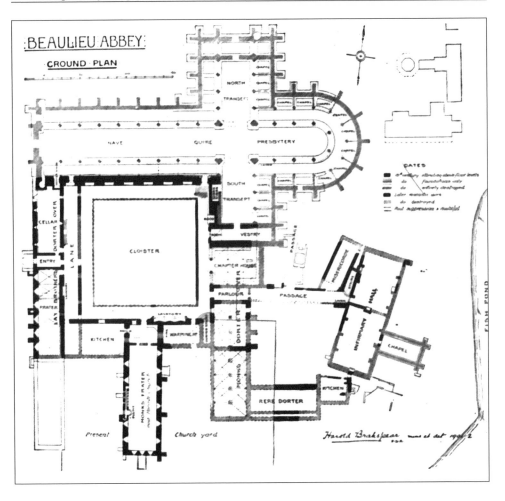

BEAULIEU ABBEY:
GROUND PLAN

33   *Beaulieu Abbey was the first of a series of Cistercian monasteries founded by the English royal family in*
      the thirteenth century. Although the refectory and a part of the west range survive, the remainder of the
      plan is only known from the excavation of its low walls and foundations (Brakspear).

in 1164 by Robert fitz Stephen the Constable of Cardigan Castle that marked a change. Rhys ap Gruffudd, prince of Deheubarth overran and recovered Ceridigion the following year and immediately took over the patronage of Strata Florida and also became a generous patron of Whitland. He began the construction of the permanent monastic buildings, the eastern parts of the church being first occupied in 1201. The Cistercians were an international movement who offered no threat to the Welsh. Indeed, it was from this moment that the Cistercian colonisation of Wales took off. In 1170, Whitland established a daughter house at Strata Marcella at the invitation of Owain ap Gruffudd, prince of Powys; and another in 1176 at Cwmhir on land granted by Cadwallon ap Madog, prince of Ceri and Maelienydd. Strata Florida established colonies at

34   *The early thirteenth-century chevet of radiating chapels at Croxden survives only as fragment of the first
chapel on the north side, though the plan of the structure can be recovered from its foundations (author).*

Llantarnam in 1179 with the support of Hywel ap Iorweth, lord of Caerleon, and
at Aberconwy in 1186. This latter house gained the support of the princes of
Gwynedd who aspired to be princes of all of Wales, particularly Llywelyn ap
Iorwerth, and it was to become the mausoleum of that dynasty. With Edward I's
defeat of Welsh independence in 1182-3, it was not without significance that the
abbey was destroyed and removed to Maenan to make way for the castle and town
of Conwy. Support of the Welsh dynasties could have its problems. In 1212, in
spite of his support of the Cistercians in England, King John ordered the
destruction of Strata Florida because it harboured his enemies and particularly
Llywelyn ap Iorweth. It was only saved by the king's inability to mount an
expedition and he had to settle for a fine of £800 which crippled the community
for the next four decades. The monks of Strata Florida became, unsurprisingly,
significant custodians of the Welsh cultural traditions.

In Scotland, the first Cistercian foundations had been directed by King David
who developed a particular affection for the White Monks. Undoubtedly, his
friendship with Aelred of Rievaulx had something to do with his support. There
was, however, a political dimension, similar to that which was later to develop in
Wales. In 1136, David declared his support for the Empress Matilda in her claim
for the English throne on the death of Henry I. He invaded the north of England,
seizing Northumberland and Cumbria, and was only prevented from extending
his control over Durham and Yorkshire by his defeat at the Battle of the Standard

fought near Northallerton in 1138. He never gave up his ambition to redraw the Anglo-Scottish border further to the south, and he certainly used his Cistercian connections to influence areas he did not directly control. In 1150, with his son Henry, he founded the abbey of Holmcultram in Cumbria, bringing the founding community from Melrose, to cement his control over the area.

Changing styles

From the 1190s, it is clear that the White Monks had evolved their liturgies to the point that the architectural models of the earlier twelfth century were no longer suited to their needs, and there was a concerted attempt to rebuild their churches, or at least their eastern parts. That this did not always happen is in itself significant, and churches like Kirkstall, Roche, Louth Park, and Sawtry retained their short aisleless presbyteries until the suppression. This plan, after all, represented the early vigour of the order, and it is perhaps significant that it was retained by most of the houses established in Wales and Scotland, and by second-tier daughter houses. Being less influenced by their patrons, and being generally less well endowed, necessity may very well have been the source of their virtue. Wealth certainly seems to have been the spur in some cases.

The Fountains chronicle contains an interesting comment dating from about 1205. The monks complained that their choir and presbytery were too dark and too cramped for their numbers, and suggested that it was not fitting for its purpose. In 1209, work began on its replacement, a four bay aisled presbytery of elaborate if restrained design (**35**), copied almost directly from the recently completed presbytery at Jervaulx. It was simply a house for the high altar, and in spite of the monks' concern, their choir stayed where it had always been, in the east end of the nave and the crossing. Completed by 1220, it was then extended with the addition of an eastern transept, the Chapel of Nine Altars, a unique building in the order which was designed to show Fountains' status as the mother house of a major family (**col. pl 12**). This new work maintained the two-storey elevation of the earlier nave and transepts, showing that there was no intention to replace them with a taller building in due course.

Fountains was not alone in its aspirations, for Waverley, which had not replaced its first stone church, began rebuilding in 1204, starting with an aisled presbytery of five bays and an eastern aisle containing chapels (**36**). In this, Waverley was following the example of its mother-house of Cîteaux which had completed its third church in 1193 to a similar plan. Only a few fragments of the Waverley church survive, but it was clearly a monumental building , designed by Dan William, rector of Broadwater, and not completed until 1278, partly as a result of the relative poverty of this mother house.

In the 1220s, Rievaulx followed Fountains in rebuilding its presbytery, and chose to build an aisled presbytery of seven bays with a three-storey elevation which is virtually indistinguishable from the presbytery the Benedictines were

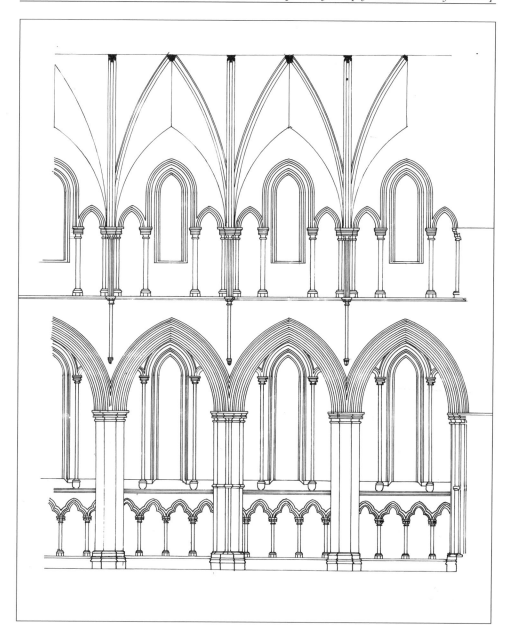

35   *The new presbytery at Fountains retained the two storey elevation of the old church, but brought a new lightness and verticality to the building. Although its arcades collapsed and were cleared away in the eighteenth century, enough fragments have been recovered to reconstruct its elevation (Harrison).*

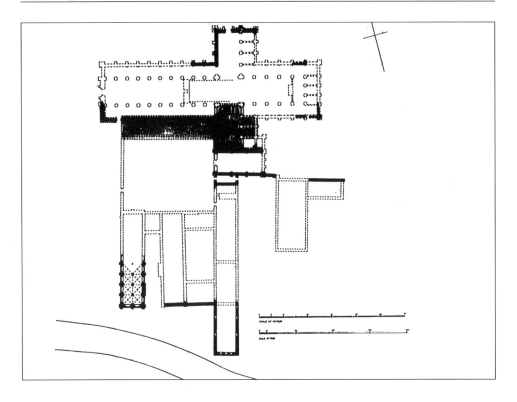

36   The church at Waverley, not begun until 1204, marked a new departure for the White Monks. Designed by William of Broadwater it was not constrained by the existence of an earlier major church, and its planning reflected the needs and aspirations of the community in the early thirteenth century (after Brakspear).

building at Whitby at the same time (**col. pl. 13-15**). Vaulted throughout and with a wealth of fine architectural detail, it represented a departure for the Cistercians in Britain, the first church to be raised to house a shrine, that of Abbot Aelred. Although the transepts were rebuilt, and a new crossing tower with bells was added when the new presbytery was raised, the old late romanesque nave was retained for the lay brethren and there is no evidence that it was ever intended to be replaced. The result was a nave which was much lower than the presbytery and transepts and one which was distinctly old fashioned. It is hardly surprising that the monks moved their choir into the new building, but it also underlines the class difference between them and the lay brothers, something that Aelred would not have tolerated.

If Rievaulx was remodelled to serve as a shrine house and to support new liturgies, it was not typical of the churches that were to be built from new in the early thirteenth century. Strata Florida had been built to a Bernardine plan in the 1190s, and it was this plan which was retained when Valle Crucis was begun in the first quarter of the thirteenth century. The church at Valle Crucis (**37; col. pl. 17**) was largely complete by the late 1240s, a short, square presbytery , shallow

37   *The church at Valle Crucis, built in the first half of the thirteenth century, though it used up-to-date architectural detailing retained the mid-twelfth-century 'Bernardine' plan with a short, aisleless presbytery. The rubble walling would have been hidden by plaster and the windows filled with grisaille glass (Cadw).*

transepts with two eastern chapels, a low crossing tower, and an aisled nave of five bays, when it was damaged in a serious fire and repaired. The same is true of Cleeve Abbey, where the church begun about 1200 and completed apart from the nave by 1230 was built to a classic Bernardine design.

At Stratford Langthorne in Essex, the presbytery of the great Bernardine church of the mid-to-late twelfth century was taken down and replaced by a new eastern arm which was still being built in 1241 when the abbot was licensed to bring stone from London (**38**). Here, the model was that of Byland and Abbey Dore, with an eastern aisle with four chapels and a four bay presbytery almost 20m long. Stratford was a wealthy monastery and could afford to keep up with fashion, even if the new presbytery was not exactly the latest design. What we do not know is what its elevations looked like, for it was almost totally destroyed in the eighteenth century when even its foundations were dug out for reuse. Lying just to the east of London, however, it is likely to have embraced the latest metropolitan fashions. A clue to its appearance might be found in Henry III's abbey of Netley in Hampshire, founded from Beaulieu in 1239 Bishop Peter des Roches, and

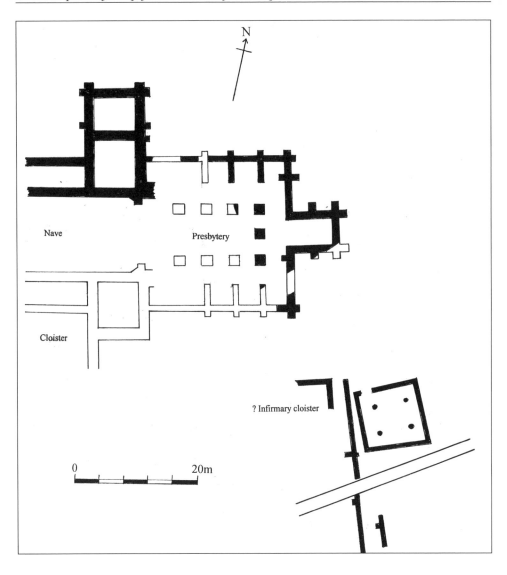

N

Nave

Presbytery

Cloister

? Infirmary cloister

0   20m

38   *The plan of the eastern parts of the church at Stratford Langthorne, extended in the 1240s, has been recovered by excavation (after MoLAS).*

completed by the King from 1251. Henry was almost certainly responsible for the building of the eastern parts of the church, for his name (H . DI . GRA . REX . ANGL.) is carved into the base of the north-eastern crossing pier.

The church (**39**) had a two-storey elevation throughout, with a presbytery of four bays and no eastern ambulatory, shallow transepts with two eastern chapels, and a nave of eight bays. It was vaulted throughout, and lit by two and three-light windows. The east window has some of the earliest tracery in Britain, though this

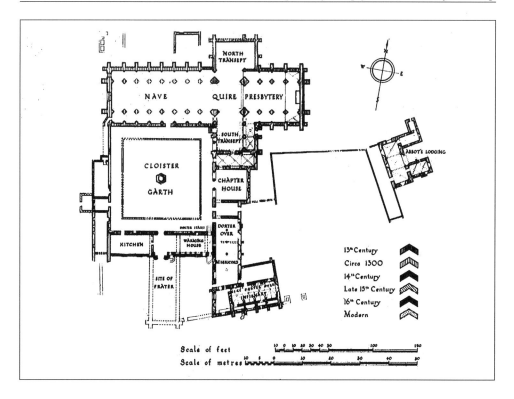

NORTH TRANSEPT

NAVE QUIRE PRESBYTERY

SOUTH TRANSEPT

ABBOT'S LODGING

CLOISTER GARTH

CHAPTER HOUSE

KITCHEN

WARMING HOUSE

DORTER OVER

MISERICORD

SITE OF FRATER

13ᵗʰ Century	
Circa 1300	
14ᵗʰ Century	
Late 15ᵗʰ Century	
16ᵗʰ Century	
Modern	

Scale of feet
Scale of metres

39   *Netley Abbey, largely built under Henry III's patronage in the mid-thirteenth-century, provides a typical example of Cistercian development at a time when the order was no longer expanding.*

has more to do with the use of royal masons than the monks' own aspirations. The high altar was placed against the east wall of the presbytery, showing that eastern chapels were not provided in the main vessel, though they were in the aisles. The cloister ranges which are contemporary with the building of this church provide a convenient snapshot of Cistercian development in the middle years of the thirteenth century, with an east and south range little changed in either scale or planning from those completed at Sawley some 50 years earlier. There was, however, only a tiny west range that did not extend as far north of the church. Clearly, by as early as the mid-thirteenth century, lay brothers were no longer playing a central role in the economy of the house and their accommodation had been drastically scaled down as a result. Similar developments can be seen elsewhere, though not as early as at Netley. At Cleeve, for instance, a short west range was provided in the later thirteenth century, and at Rievaulx, the west range was drastically shortened in the late fourteenth century.

The foundation of Hailes in 1246 by Richard, Earl of Cornwall marks the next stage in Cistercian development (**40**). Again, the founding community came from

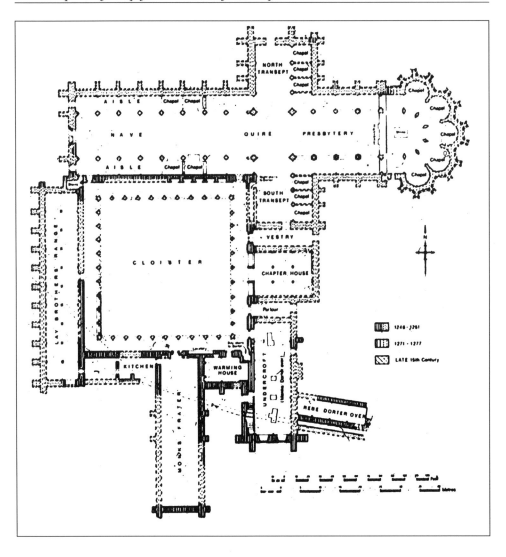

40   *The royal foundation of Hailes which housed 20 monks and 10 lay brothers drawn from Beaulieu
became a famous pilgrimage centre when it acquired a phial of the Holy Blood in 1270.*

Beaulieu, and there are, not surprisingly, similarities in the planning of Hailes, Netley, and Beaulieu itself. Building probably began before the settlement of the site, and was sufficiently complete for the church and cloister buildings to be dedicated in 1251. Once more a modest west range was planned, with sufficient space for some 80 lay brothers. Again, the church appears to have had a two storey elevation, an aisled presbytery of four bays and a nave of eight bays, and it shared the traceried windows of Netley. In 1270, though, the community was given a remarkable relic, a phial of the Holy Blood, authenticated by the Patriarch of

Jerusalem (later Pope Urban IV) himself. To house the relic, the east wall of the presbytery was taken down, the presbytery extended one bay to the east, and a chevet or corona of five radiating chapels built to ring the new shrine. The model for this new east end was Henry III's new church at Westminster, a building that had already influenced the development of Beaulieu, and was to be copied again in Edward I's new abbey of Vale Royal a few years later.

At Beaulieu, the radiating chapels had been enclosed within a semi-circular apse that harked back to the eastern arm of Clairvaux, but at Hailes and Vale Royal no attempt was made to hide the exuberance of the design. The Holy Blood of Hailes rapidly became a national shrine, with pilgrims flocking to the abbey, perhaps the first instance of the public being welcomed into a Cistercian church in Britain. The shrines of abbots William and Aelred at Rievaulx, built in 1215 and the 1220s, were in contrast were objects of the devotion of the community, never intended for public gaze. Interestingly, this development at Hailes is contemporary with the first lay burials in Cistercian churches, something the Cistercians had opposed strongly into the thirteenth century. It was an admission that patrons required something more than spiritual salvation for their generosity, and marked the first real move by the Cistercians back towards the world they had shunned in the twelfth century.

Roughly contemporary with the coming of the Holy Blood to Hailes was the founding of the New Abbey in south-west Scotland from Dundrennan by Devorgilla, widow of John Balliol, in 1273. Designed as her burial place and that of her husband's heart, the community soon adopted the name of Sweetheart, a name that has endured. Although the Bernardine plan had already begun to be replaced by more developed model of Byland at Newbattle and Kinloss, it was retained at Sweetheart, together with the two storey elevation. The church (**41; col. pl. 16**) survives substantially complete, with its low crossing tower and three-light clerestorey windows. The presbytery was lit by traceried windows, though the west gable of the nave was unusually treated with three graduated lancet windows and a rose window set within the outline of a massive but otherwise blind window. The use of a triplet of lights and a rose window can be traced back to Fountains and Kirkstall in the early 1160s and was a standard design for great Bernardine churches. Its survival into the late thirteenth century is hardly remarkable, for the great northern abbeys retained their twelfth-century fenestration until the late fifteenth century. More surprising is the galilee porch against the west wall of the nave, normally a place of lay burial, which had already gone out of fashion in England. The cloister ranges provided for the monks followed the standard Cistercian plan, but it would appear that no west range was ever built, and the west side of the cloister was closed by a single wall. Either the lay brothers remained in temporary quarters within the abbey, or they were all stationed within granges. Wherever they were, their numbers cannot have been substantial, a further confirmation that they played a decreasing role in the order in Britain an the thirteenth century came to a close.

Perhaps the clearest example of how the White Monks' monasteries were

41   *Devorgilla Balliol's church at the New or Sweetheart Abbey was built like Hailes as a mausoleum church, a new departure for the Cistercians who had previously refused to allow lay burials in their churches (author).*

changing comes from Tintern. Here, the first stone church survived into the later thirteenth century, though its replacement had been planned from the second quarter of the century. Rebuilding began with the cloister ranges, starting with a new refectory. Its cloister wall was set back from the line of the twelfth century north range, showing that an enlarge cloister was planned, an acknowledgement that conditions were cramped and that Tintern was at last raising buildings of a style and scale that indicated its rank and wealth. The new refectory (**42**) was a remarkable building lit by paired two-light windows with plate tracery, with a large kitchen to the west and a warming house with a central hearth and chimney to the east. The east range was then modernised, with a new chapter house that extended two bays to the east of the range, and a parlour to its north. The old day room was given new windows and converted to the noviciate, and an abbot's house was attached to the east end of the latrine block. Tintern was clearly bringing itself up to date rapidly. Finally, the west range was rebuilt, to the west of its original site, towards the middle of the century. It was initially a small building only some 40m long though it was later extended to 60m, again suggesting a falling off in the number of lay brethren.

In about 1269, work began on a new church that was completed in 1301 with the support of Roger Bigod III, earl of Norfolk and lord of Chepstow. The new

42   *The new refectory at Tintern was begun in the1320s, an elaborate building with plate tracery windows (author).*

church, which was built around its predecessor, was a remarkable building that still stands substantially complete apart from the north arcade of the church which fell in the late eighteenth century. It was vaulted throughout with a restrained two-storey elevation and traceried windows (**43**). In spite of falling numbers, the nave was still the church of the lay brethren, and the walls that supported their stalls remain, an integral part of the inner face of the nave piers, a feature first noted at Byland in the 1170s. The lay brothers' church was divided from the monks' church to the east by a stone rood screen two bays west of the crossing. One bay further east was the pulpitum screen which survived until the mid nineteenth century and which has recently been identified among the collection of loose stone recovered from the clearance of the site (**44**). Its elaboration might seem out of place in a Cistercian church, but it is not unique. Similar screens have been identified at Abbey Dore and at Rievaulx.

The loss of fittings, and of wall finishes, gives an inaccurate impression of the interior of all great churches, particularly in one as complete as Tintern. These great churches were divided by screens and never seen as an open space, they were full of light, filtered by the late thirteenth century through coloured glass

43   *The new church at Tintern retained the two-storey elevation so typical of the Cistercians, and was vaulted throughout. The great traceried window at the west end of the nave was designed for pictorial glass, which had begun to appear in Cistercian churches from the end of the thirteenth century. The nave piers seen here rise from the wall that supported the lay brothers' stalls (author).*

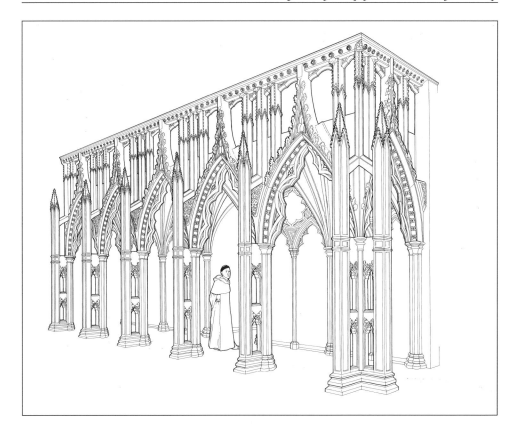

44 The pulpitum screen at Tintern can be reconstructed from its elements cleared from the site in the mid-nineteenth century (Jones-Jenkins for Cadw, Welsh Historic Monuments (Crown Copyright)).

windows, and their walls were plastered and painted. The floors were covered with tiles, either in mosaic patterns in houses like Byland, Meaux, Fountains, Rievaulx, Melrose, or Newbattle, or patterned tiles as at Bordesley, Netley, Hailes, and Tintern. From the later thirteenth century, when patronal burial was permitted in Cistercian churches, they began to fill with fine tombs which were also painted (**45**).

The fourteenth century and the demise of the lay brethren

By the early years of the fourteenth century, the Cistercians had begun to experience a sea-change which was to have a dramatic effect on their development. They had, by and large, over-extended themselves in the late thirteenth century, living on the income of extensively farmed estates without the wisdom of the late twelfth and early thirteenth century abbots who had developed them. Even Fountains, one of the richest houses in Britain, had found itself

45   *Burial effigy of Henry Percy, Lord of Alnwick, which was placed in the centre of the presbytery at Fountains in 1315 (Hayfield). Similar effigies are known from Abbey Dore, Deer, Dundrennan, Furness, Hailes, Jervaulx, Kirkstead, Margam, Neath, Rievaulx and Strata Florida.*

seriously in debt in the late thirteenth century. Many houses had specialised in wool production, because their estates were on marginal land that was ideal for sheep, and they had entered into contracts with Italian wool-merchants, often selling several years crop in advance to fund building campaigns and further land purchases. In 1280, there was a major outbreak of sheep scab that decimated flocks, and Fountains, which ran 15,000 sheep on its granges, was suddenly faced with a major loss of income. Wool had to be bought on the open market to make up the losses, and by 1291, Fountains was in debt to the tune of £6,376, an immense sum in the late thirteenth century. Loans had even been raised on the security of the abbey itself. Fountains was not alone, and many houses were also having to retrench.

The result was a falling number of choir monks, to levels that the abbeys could support. Competition, too, for new recruits was a factor that changed Cistercian expectations. The Cistercians were no longer as popular with the land-owning classes who had supported them, and monasteries generally were feeling the competition of the new urban friaries which were drawing away potential recruits and patrons. The first half of the fourteenth century was one of general retrenchment for the order in Britain, made worse in the north of England by the incursion of the Scots after the battle of Bannockburn in 1314. Granges were burned, crops destroyed, and the northern monasteries were obliged to provide men and materials to support the English army. Fountains was even occupied by the Scots in 1318, and Rievaulx was looted in 1322 when the English army was routed nearby. In Wales, the earlier campaigns of Edward I left many Welsh Cistercian houses and their estates open to attack between 1270 and 1290, with similar results. Renewed war with Scotland in 1329, after earlier defeat, left the English in their turn to ravage the estates of the Scottish monasteries in the borders for another twenty years. When recovery began to look possible, the pandemic of the Black Death hit Britain in 1348-9, decimating the population both outside and within the monastic world.

Retrenchment and uncertain times finally killed off the lay brothers as an effective part of Cistercian communities. Their choirs were removed from the naves of Cistercian churches, and their buildings were converted to other uses. Smaller numbers of choir monks also led to the replanning of their ranges, and from the late fourteenth century, the gradual abandonment of their old communal ranges in favour of small households within the abbey.

Rievaulx Abbey provides one of the clearest examples of the re-ordering of a Cistercian community in the course of the fourteenth century. The mid-twelfth and early thirteenth-century church and cloister ranges had survived unaltered into the second quarter of the fourteenth century, even though the lay brothers had all but disappeared. By 1340, the choir had been removed from the nave which became an open space, and once the walls which had supported the lay brothers stalls had been removed the aisles which had provided passages around the lay brothers' church were divided up into chapels (**col. pl. 18**). This also happened at Fountains where the evidence is now less clear, Hailes, Byland, and

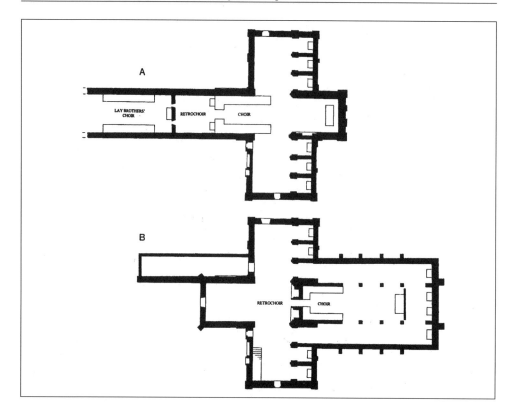

46   *The unaisled mid-to-late twelfth-century church at Sawley (a) was substantially rebuilt in the late*
     fourteenth century (b), with a new aisled presbytery. The greater part of the nave was demolished,
     leaving only a stub to form a porch.

Jervaulx. At Roche, the nave was used for lay burial on a substantial scale, with the chantry chapels of rich patronal families, and the simpler graves of members of the confraternity of the abbey. The nave at Rievaulx was clearly still of importance to the community, because in the later fourteenth century its clerestorey windows were renewed and the west front was remodelled. Perhaps as at Fountains it was now used as processional space by the community. The rood screen was moved eastwards to the western arch of the crossing as part of this re-ordering, and the nave floor was retiled. In the early fifteenth century, Abbot Henry Burton was buried in the eastern chapel of the south aisle, which probably served as his chantry, showing that the nave was still regarded as an important space.

Late Cistercian churches are not common, for in most cases, the White Monks were content to modernise their twelfth- and thirteenth-century churches. In one instance, at Sawley (**6, 46**), the twelfth-century nave was demolished in the 1370s, and a new church built for the monks to the east of their old presbytery. The original twelfth-century presbytery formed the nucleus of the first bay of the new

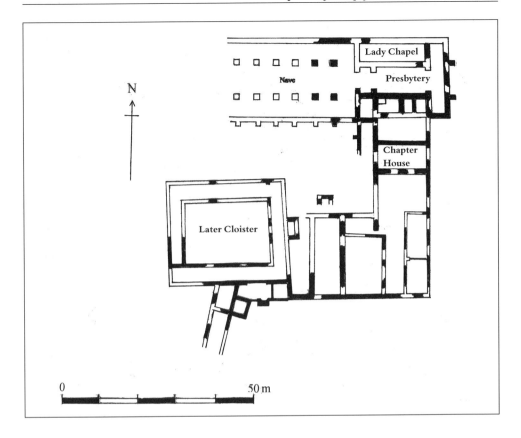

N

Lady Chapel

Nave

Presbytery

Chapter House

Later Cloister

0   50 m

47   *Excavation on the site of the old Royal Mint on Tower Hill has revealed the greater part of the ground*
      plan of the Abbey of St Mary Graces (after MoLAS).

church which was an aisled building of five bays with a series of chapels in the
eastern bay. Between the eastern crossing piers is the pulpitum which enclosed the
monks' choir, with small chapels to either side of its central door. The nave was
demolished apart from its south wall which enclosed the cloister and eastern bays,
and a new wall was built two bays west of the crossing. Essentially, the eastern part
of the old nave and the transepts were little more than a porch, used for the
Sunday procession and lay burials.

The foundation of the last Cistercian abbey in Britain in 1350 on a plague
cemetery to the north-east of the Tower of London, an unusual urban setting for
the White Monks, provides an indication of what sort of church the Cistercians
might build from new in the middle years of the fourteenth century (**47**).
Completed by the 1390s, the church of St Mary Graces, which follows the plan
of mid-fourteenth-century friary churches rather than any standard Cistercian
layout, had a nave of at least seven bays with broad aisles, and initially an unaisled
choir arm of four bays that terminated in an eastern transept that appears to copy

48   *The chapter house at Rievaulx in its late medieval form. The aisle that ran around the building was removed, though the central area used by the monks was unaltered (author).*

the chapel of Nine Altars at Fountains. A tower was placed over the western bay of the eastern arm, which probably served the same function as the 'walking place' of a friary church. If we did not know that this church had been built for a community drawn from Beaulieu it would not be obvious that it was a Cistercian church. By 1442, an aisle had been added to the south side of the presbytery, containing a series of chapels, and in the second half of the fifteenth century, a Lady Chapel was built on the north side effectively adding a second aisle. Anthony van den Wingaerde's panorama of London drawn in about 1543, just before the church was demolished, shows a great rectangular church, with no transepts and a central tower. Excavation also revealed the domestic buildings of the abbey. The earliest phase of these appears to follow the standard Cistercian plan, with a sacristy, chapter house, and dormitory in the east range, and a south range with a small warming house, north-south refectory, and kitchen. No west range has been found and it may never have existed. The scale of these buildings was commensurate with a small community, originally only an abbot and six monks enjoying only a small endowment. They were, however, to be replaced within a century by a completely new arrangement, where the refectory was to become the dormitory, the kitchen a new latrine block, and a new detached cloister, with warming house, refectory, and kitchen attached to its south side, built.

Elsewhere, where the monks were constrained by old but substantial buildings,

49   *The new refectory at Cleeve as it was early this century when it still retained a wall-painting of Christ Crucified on its east wall (James).*

the mid-to-late fourteenth century saw contraction, with redundant buildings demolished and large buildings reduced in size. At Rievaulx, where this is particularly apparent, the southern halves of the west and east ranges were demolished, together with a substantial part of the monks' latrine. The vast chapter house was shorn of its aisle and its arcade blocked up with new masonry (**48**). In 1381, there were only an abbot, 14 monks, and three lay brothers at Rievaulx, and the buildings were simply too big for them. Although the shortened dormitory is substantially ruined, it is apparent that some of its windows were enlarged, and the building was divided up into individual cells, perhaps of more than one room. A similar development can be seen at Byland, where the infirmary was torn down and replaced by a range of what can only be described as bachelor apartments, suites of two rooms, one with a fireplace and a latrine, where the monks could enjoy a degree of privacy never available in the great communal dormitories. How widespread this sort of development was is not easy to determine because of the poor survival of evidence for internal partitioning in surviving cloister ranges. It is unlikely, however, that houses of the standing of Rievaulx and Byland would be out of step with other houses of the order. To a certain extent, this is confirmed by Abbot David Juyner's rebuilding of the south cloister range at Cleeve in the 1450s. The purpose of this work was to provide a new refectory (**49**) at first floor level and parallel to the south cloister range. The

50   *The living room of one of the small apartments beneath the refectory at Cleeve (English Heritage).*

ground floor of the range was made up of two small apartments, each with a living room (**50**) with a fireplace and a bed-chamber with a latrine. Because they could only be reached from the cloister they must surely be for senior members of the community.

The last great church to be built in Britain by the White Monks was the church at Melrose, occasioned by Richard II's burning of the abbey in 1385. So serious was the damage, that an almost complete rebuilding had to be undertaken, an enterprise which began in the early fifteenth century and was not completed before the church was again destroyed by the English in 1545 (**51**). Extended slightly to the east of the original Bernardine church, it repeated its plan and two storey elevations, though its elevations were enlivened with the late Decorated and Perpendicular architecture of the north of England and literally covered with sculpture. The nave, which was never completed, had an outer or second aisle on the south side which contained eight chapels divided by masonry walls and covered with vaults. The interior of the church was as elaborate as the exterior; the monks' stalls were highly carved and commissioned from Cornelius de Aeltre, master of the joiners' guild of Bruges, and finally delivered in 1441 after a series of delays. The nave chapels, too, were fitted with Flemish screens, panelling, and retables, financed through the sale of Melrose wool through Ghent and Bruges. Clearly no expense was spared to provide the premier Cistercian abbey of Scotland with a fitting church of the latest design.

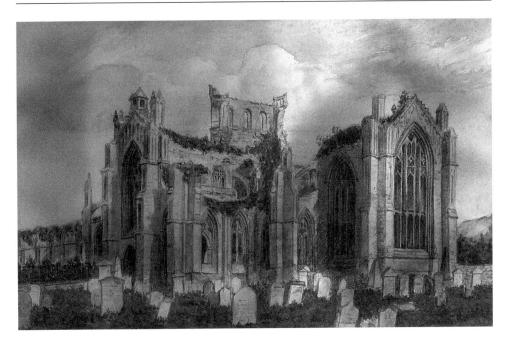

51   *The presbytery and south transept of the fifteenth century church at Melrose, a watercolour sketch of the ruins before they were conserved for display (author).*

The later Middle Ages saw the elevation of Cistercian abbots to the same social level as their contemporaries in other orders. Traditionally, they had occupied small houses which were associated in some way with the dormitory, maintaining some respect of the injunction for the abbot to sleep with the rest of the community. From the late fourteenth century, however, it is apparent that rank required the abbot to maintain a house which was in keeping with his status. With small communities housed in barn-like buildings, it was not difficult to find space to develop a new house. The abbot of Sawley converted the west range of the cloister to a new house in the late fourteenth century (**6**), with a substantial first-floor hall with an oriel window, a chamber, and chapel which was indistinguishable from the house of a Benedictine or Augustinian superior at the same date. As the person nominally responsible for the abbey's estates, outside the abbey he enjoyed the status of an earl. His new house was simply one of the trappings of his rank. In comparison, the abbots of Fountains and Rievaulx, presidents of much greater standing, were initially content to maintain the substantial halls and chambers they had already, and to maintain their connection, however tenuous, with the dormitory.

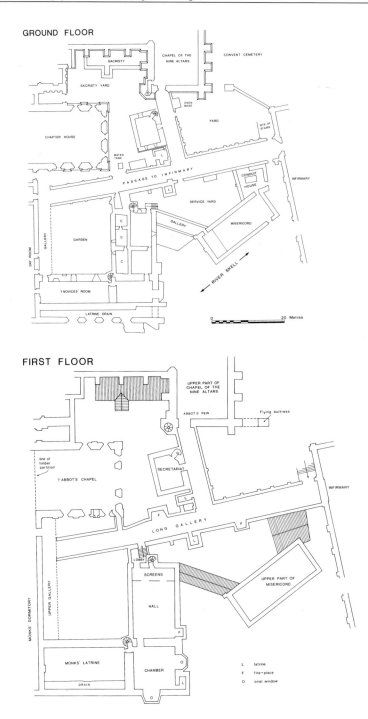

52   *The buildings that comprised the abbot's house at Fountains all lie between the east range of the cloister and the infirmary. The plan of the upper storey is reconstructed from the outline apparent in the basement storey of the buildings.*

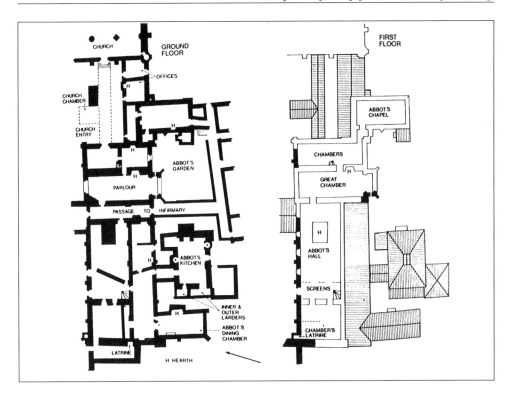

53   Abbot John Burton's house at Rievaulx can be reconstructed from its surviving ruins and a series of surveys made in 1538-9 when it was still complete.

At Fountains, this did not prevent the abbot encroaching on the surrounding buildings (**52**) as the size of his household increased. Abbot Walter of Coxwold appears to have begun the development of the abbot's apartments in the 1320s or 30s, substantially rebuilding an earlier house. The accommodation was all at first-floor level with a substantial hall and chamber, built over a basement that contained three prison cells. As the numbers of choir monks reduced in the later fourteenth century, the wall between the hall and chamber was demolished to create an new hall 16.2m long and 10m wide. A new chamber was then created in the east end of the monks' latrines.

In the fifteenth century, the abbot began to enlarge the house again, probably in the time of John Darnton. The old gallery that had linked the thirteenth-century infirmary hall to the east range was substantially strengthened to provide a long gallery at first floor level, with flanking fire-places and latrines, the very latest fashion in the greatest laymen's houses. A bridge from this gallery led into that part of the monks' dormitory that lay over the chapter house, and which was converted to a chapel for the abbot. Again the abbot was expanding his house at the expense of the convent. John Darnton also built a refectory for the infirmary, the *misericordia* in which meat could be eaten by the community and not simply

54   The north range of Forde Abbey, with Abbot Chard's house on the left (James).

*55   The late medieval abbot's house at Valle Crucis occupied the northern half of what had been the monks'
dormitory (Jones-Jenkins for Cadw, Welsh Historic Monuments (Crown Copyright)).*

56   Abbot Huby's bell-tower at Fountains, completed in the 1520s (English Heritage).

the sick and old monks. However, he linked the misericord to the screens passage of his own hall, and not directly to the infirmary showing very clearly that he regarded it as a second hall for his own house. Marmaduke Huby, the last great abbot of Fountains continued this expansion in the first quarter of the sixteenth century, adding impressive fireplaces and bay windows to the house and building a two-storey office to house his secretariat. Although the house created by Darnton and Huby was somewhat irregular in its plan, it was impressive both in terms of its size and elaboration.

The abbot of Rievaulx was content to occupy a rebuilt version of Aelred's original house until the very end of the fifteenth century. Then he took over the great twelfth-century infirmary, and created one of the largest abbot's houses in Britain (**53**). Again, the principal accommodation was at first-floor level, with the hall occupying four full bays of the old hall, with a great central fireplace and a screens passage. To the north, a cross-wing was inserted with a great oriel window in its east wall, the abbot's parlour at ground floor level and his great chamber at the level of the hall. North of this were closets and the abbot's study, and the infirmary chapel converted to the abbot's use. The old abbot's house to the west was converted into a fashionable long gallery, the 'long house' of sixteenth-century surveys, reached from the upper end of the hall. South of the hall were more chambers, perhaps for senior members of the abbot's household and his secretariat. On the ground floor, to the east, was the old misericord, now the abbot's private dining chamber. The old and sick were displaced to a new and somewhat smaller infirmary converted from service buildings to the east. Between the two infirmaries was the old infirmary kitchen, again taken over by the abbot and remodelled.

Abbot Thomas Chard of Forde remodelled the refectory range of his abbey in the early sixteenth century, and built to the west of it a new house for himself (**54**). His hall, which survives intact, was entered from the south by a tower porch, and had a chamber block at its west end. Although it has been modified, Chard's house is the finest Cistercian abbot's house to survive, an essay in late Perpendicular architecture completed just before the suppression of his abbey.

What the abbots of great abbeys did was paralleled by their lesser brothers elsewhere. At Valle Crucis, the northern half of the monks' dormitory was taken over by the abbot to provide him with a new hall (**55**), and a room was created over the sacristy on the south side of the south transept to accommodate his chamber. Because the door to the hall was inserted into the cloister wall and cut through the line of the cloister roof it would appear that the cloister alleys had already gone out of use and the eastern alley at least demolished.

The impression given by the growth of abbots' houses at the expense of the community is that Cistercian monasteries were generally in decline while the power and social standing of the abbot was steadily rising. While the later is certainly true, the former is not necessarily the case. Numbers of monks had begun to rise again in the late fifteenth century, marking a slight renaissance that was to continue until 1536. Powerful abbots were also great builders and administrators. Marmaduke Huby of Fountains completed the restoration of his church begun by his predecessor John Darnton, supplying new choir stalls and building a great bell-tower that still bears his name and is decorated with his motto *Soli Deo Honor et Gloria* ('Only to God be the honour and glory') (**56**), and left his mark on every part of the abbey. Whether the intention was simply to honour God, or to show what a successful abbot Huby was and what status he had brought to his abbey is questionable. Others like Abbot William Dovell of Cleeve who rebuilt the inner gatehouse there in the early sixteenth century were more Cistercian in their motives. Still mindful of the order's obligation to charity, he placed above the gate an inscription: *Porta patens esto, nulli claudaris honesto* ('gate be open, shut to no honest person').

5 The Cistercian economy

Almost all medieval monasteries were sustained by landed estates that made up their endowment, the gifts of the founder or subsequent patrons, or purchased from the cash revenues of the house. By the time the English and Welsh monasteries were suppressed in 1536-40 it has been estimated that they controlled between a tenth and a seventh of the available land. Central to the Benedictine rule was the assumption that monasteries would be self-sufficient, providing for their own needs, those of their guests, and the poor to whom the monks owed charity. Any surplus would fund building or buy further land and develop it. By the tenth century, it was common for monasteries to hold substantial estates. The royal foundation of Bury St Edmunds, for instance, founded by Cnut in 1020 to atone for his father Sweyn Forkbeard's harrying of an earlier community of priests on the site, was endowed with a royal estate that equates to modern West Suffolk. The Benedictines and Cluniacs were content to manage their estates in the same way as laymen, with tied labour or bondsmen who were gifted with the land, or by tenanting land for service in the same way as lay landowners. They were also prepared to hold churches, taking the greater proportion of the tithes and fees, always a profitable proposition, while finding a priest to serve the parish.

From the first, the White Monks rejected any dependence on feudal labour or on the gift of parish churches, claiming that this brought them into contact with the outside world and would threaten their independence. Underlying this was the requirement for the monks themselves to undertake manual labour. The *Exordium Parvum* describes how the first monks of Cîteaux cultivated their fields with their own hands, and they continued to work the fields at harvest time even when they had developed armies of lay brothers. Certainly, by the time Stephen Harding become abbot of the New Monastery, the community included both lay brethren who took monastic vows and *laici* or paid labourers who had not, for both appear in the initial letters of the *Moralia in Job*, one of the earliest books to survive from the Cîteaux library (**col. pl. 2**). If the white monks were to dispense with the services of laymen they had to provide an alternative, and the development of the lay brothers as a self-contained and directed labour force was a brilliant solution. As well as offering a religious life to the uneducated labouring classes it enabled the Cistercians to move into areas of marginal land where there was little or no existing population and to colonise it with workers they could

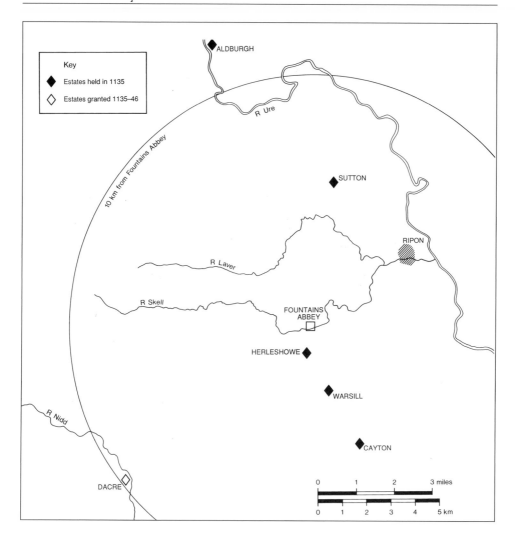

57   *The earliest estates of Fountains Abbey all lay within 6 miles (10km) of the abbey, and show that the community had already decided where it wanted to develop its earliest granges.*

trust and who were as clear in their objectives as the monks were themselves.

Initially, the first Cistercians in Britain were content with little more than land on which to build an abbey and sufficient land to support the community. In 1131, Walter Espec of Helmsley granted to Abbot Bernard of Clairvaux the vills of Griff and Tilleston with nine carucates (about 1200 acres; 486ha) of cultivated land, effectively the lands of two villages, to form the basis of a new abbey. As Rievaulx had been carefully planned it is fair to assume that the endowment was designed with a founding community in mind. The only other early foundation for which we have any information is Fountains, which Archbishop Thurstan planted in the 'wood of Herleshowe', with some 260 acres (105ha) at Sutton to the north of the abbey and 200 acres (81ha) at Herleshowe, a much smaller endowment. In both cases, the intention was only to provide initial support while the abbey was established, and the intention was that as the new communities settled in they would attract both new recruits and other gifts of land. At Rievaulx, Walter Espec increased his initial endowment to include a vast block of land the comprised all of Bilsdale and the moorland above it in 1145, and the abbey's charter book, compiled in the later twelfth century, lists other donations granted by that time; gifts from the king, the bishop of Durham, local barons and knights, that totalled some 6000 acres (2430ha). It was the rapid acquisition of land that enabled Abbot William to start raising permanent buildings in the 1140s and to start the laborious task of constructing estates centred on farm centres or granges which would be managed by lay brothers. The very name grange comes from the Latin *grangia,* meaning a granary, an indication of the agricultural base of the estates.

The way in which early estates were assembled remains unclear as the evidence has not often been preserved in charters. It was assumed that landowners flocked to give land to the White Monks out of charity. This was not always the case, however, as the case of Fountains demonstrates. Fountains almost failed through lack of endowment. Archbishop Thurstan was limited in the support he could give the community as his estates belonged to his diocese and not to him personally and of course he had no heir to continue his patronage. Local landowners were initially reluctant to support a community which might fail. In 1135, at the point the abbey had achieved *stabilitas* they only held their initial foundation endowment of Sutton and Herleshowe and two carucates (260 acres or 105ha) at Cayton, the gift of Eustace fitz John of Knaresborough 'for the building of the abbey'. Eleven years later, however, in the year the first permanent buildings of the abbey were burned, the monks had granges at Sutton, Cayton, Cowton Moor, Warsill, Dacre, and Aldburgh (**57**). This list hides a host of small land grants, leases and purchases and demonstrates how the community had suddenly begun to organise its estates. The grange of Warsill, for instance, was made up of lands in Bishop Thornton granted by Robert de Sartis and his wife for an annual rent of 6s 8d (33p), Gill Moor on which the abbey had established a sheep run before 1136 was bought by the abbey from de Sartis, and land at Warsill which was originally rented by the convent for half a mark of silver (33p) but later granted by Robert and his wife, probably an early form of hire purchase. In contrast, Bertram Haget gave land valued at two marks (£1.33) that formed the basis of Dacre Grange as early as 1138, and he had an interest in the Cistercian reform for his son Ralph was later to become abbot first of Kirkstall and then of Fountains in the later twelfth century. The Fountains community was trying to build up blocks of land by whatever means to form consolidated granges from about 1140.

Precisely how the Cistercians managed their economy in the middle years of the twelfth century is far from clear, but it is likely that they began as they were to

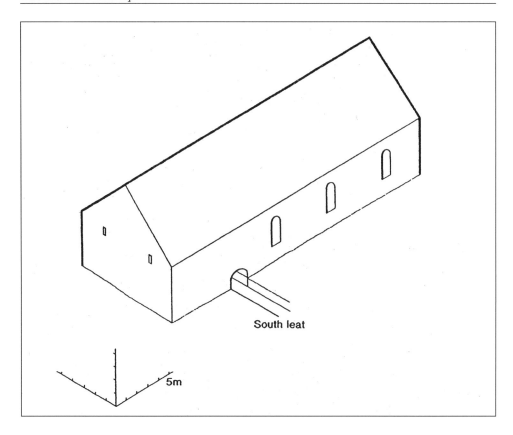

South leat

5m

58   *The 1140's mill at Fountains, now buried within a later mill dam, is the oldest Cistercian water mill to have been identified. A single-storey building, it was set over a leat taken off the river to the north which powered its single wheel.*

continue, with the abbey itself at the centre of a web of granges. Benedictine and Cluniac abbeys comprised three distinct elements, the house which comprised the church and cloister buildings, the inner court which contained the guest accommodation and service buildings like the brewhouse and bakehouse, granaries and stables, and the outer court which contained agricultural and industrial buildings. This tripartite layout had certainly been developed before the early ninth century for it appears in the St Gallen plan. However, we simply do not know what the earliest Cistercian abbeys comprised. If the house could exist without a cloister in the first phase of Clairvaux or Fountains, did other parts of the monastery have to parallel the Benedictine norm? Only one site has given the slightest clue. At Sawley, below the second phase of timber temporary buildings were a series of cobbled yards and spreads of blacksmithing waste, suggesting the presence of a forge in the late 1140s or early 1150s. Otherwise, nothing is known of the economic development of early Cistercian houses in Britain. The research has simply not been done.

The picture only begins to become clear when timber buildings were replaced in stone, and even here the evidence comes from a single site. At Fountains stone cloister ranges were being built in the early 1140s, and it is precisely at this time that the first service building was raised in what was to become the outer court of the monastery. Because it was built by Henry Murdac, a confidant of Abbot Bernard of Clairvaux, it ought to reflect continental practice of that time. Contemporary with the earliest granges of the house, this was a water mill (**58**) built over a leat on the south side of the river Skell. Initially it would appear that grain produced on the granges was brought to the abbey for processing, and as all the early granges were within 6 miles (10km) of the abbey that was quite feasible. Excavation at Fountains has also revealed waste from a tannery dating from the 1140s, demonstrating that animals were brought into the abbey itself for slaughter and that their skins were treated there. Tanning is a noxious business which must have disturbed the tranquillity of the monastery. However, the animals were sheep rather than cattle, and their skins were almost certainly being turned into vellum for the production of books, just at the time the colonies were being sent out.

If Fountains and Rievaulx have demonstrated that they have three phases of development in the monks' own buildings, they have also demonstrated that their economic development went through three stages that relate directly to the building and rebuilding of the monastery and provide a model for other houses where the basic research has yet to be done. From about 1150, both monasteries began to consolidate their estates with a degree of determination that was quite remarkable. At Rievaulx, a substantial estate (**59**) was built up between 1147 and 1188 by Abbots Aelred, Roger, and Sylvan. The principal estates lay to the north and east of the abbey, centred on the home granges of Griff, Newlathes, Bilsdale, Laskill, and Sproxton, with further granges at Hesketh, Skiplam and Pickering; to the north-west across the Hambledon Hills the granges of Angram, Crosby, Morton, and Broughton exploited holdings in the fertile Vale of Mowbray, and land in the lower Tees valley was managed from Normanby. In West Yorkshire, industrial granges were established at Fawether and Halton near Bingley and in South Yorkshire at Stainborough as early as the 1160s to exploit local deposits of iron on a vast scale. Most granges practised a mixed economy, but many also specialised. Laskill was the site of the abbey's woolhouse, a substantial masonry building that can still be traced, that was the central depot for the abbey's main cash crop. Normanby specialised in the breeding of horses and Pickering was the main centre of wool production to the east of the abbey. Low Bolton to the west managed the abbey's sheep runs between Uredale and Swaledale.

Parallel to the development of the estate was the development of the precinct of the abbey itself, and the two operations were closely connected. When Rievaulx had been established, the River Rye ran down the centre of its valley and Walter Espec only controlled the east bank. The west bank belonged to Gundreda d'Aubigny and her son Roger de Mowbray and had been granted to Byland Abbey.

59   *The estates of Rievaulx reconstructed from the abbey's late twelfth-century collection of charters.*

The area available to develop an outer court was therefore extremely limited. It was only by a series of agreements with the monks of Byland and other landowners that Rievaulx was able to divert the river (**60**) and develop a precinct of some 100 acres (40ha) . The old course of the river was retained as a leat which drove no fewer than three mills in the sixteenth century, and having control of both banks allowed the convent to control the waterflow. Rievaulx developed a precinct which is unlike that of any other order, suggesting that the Cistercians had adopted a different form of economic infrastructure to the Benedictines and Cluniacs. The greater part of the precinct comprised water meadows, and the great animal houses found elsewhere were lacking. Sixteenth century surveys show that the only agricultural buildings of any scale were those of the swinehouse, a corn mill, and a fulling mill, and the only major industrial building a water-powered forge. They also indicate that the great barns, ox-houses, and

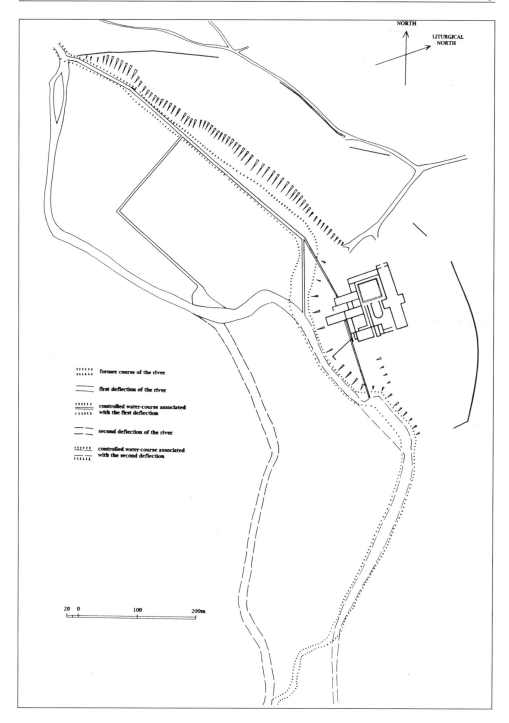

NORTH

LITURGICAL
NORTH

former course of the river

first deflection of the river

controlled water-course associated
with the first deflection

second deflection of the river

controlled water-course associated
with the second deflection

20 0   100   200m

60   *The development of the precinct at Rievaulx can be reconstructed from detailed charter evidence which
        indicate three stages of expansion as the needs of the house continued to expand (Atkins and Coppack).*

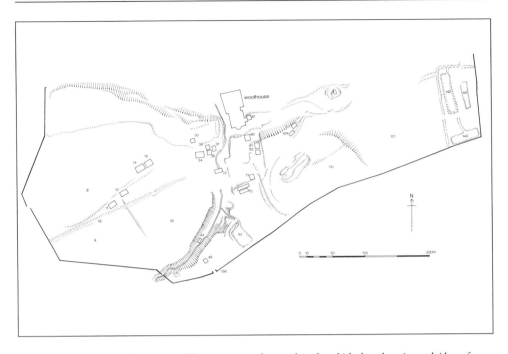

61   *The outer court of Fountains Abbey survives as clear earthworks which show how it was laid out from the middle years of the twelfth century. Apart from the great woolhouse and the mill, there were twenty one small agricultural and industrial buildings in this area, most of which comprised pasture and orchards.*

granaries lay in the home granges of Griff and Newlathes which accounted for some of the land within the precinct as part of the granges. There seems, in fact, to have been no distinction between the precinct and the home granges.

This was also the case at Fountains, where the south bank of the River Skell comprised the outer court (**61**). Here there is clear evidence for buildings, but with two exceptions they were small, with no evidence of the great barns and granaries which would be found in the outer courts of other orders. There are rare exceptions to this rule, for a thirteenth-century barn of eleven bays does survive within the precinct at Llantarnum. Apart from the mill, however, there is no evidence that the precinct began to be developed until the 1150s, when the great woolhouse was first built. The adjacent granges of Morker and Fountains Park appear to have contained the barns, animal houses, and even fish ponds that served the monastery. Indeed, the only ponds within the precinct at Fountains were header-tanks for the abbey's piped water supply, and the existence of a small stream or ghyll flowing down the side of the valley into the Skell is the reason why at least twelve small buildings including a mill (72 on **fig. 61**) were located within the precinct at that point.

Although the earthworks at Fountains reflect four centuries of development

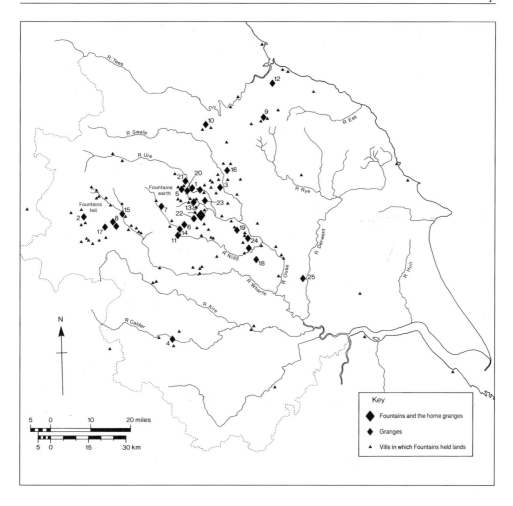

62   *The estates of Fountains Abbey as they were in 1535 were little changed from the extent they had achieved by c1180. Most of the lands lay in Yorkshire, though they also spread into Cumbria. Many of the symbols on this map conceal substantial holdings. The granges are: 1 Aldburgh, 2 Arnford, 3 Baldersby, 4 Bradley, 5 Bramley, 6 Brimham, 7 Bouthwaite, 8 Bordely, 9 Busby, 10 Cowton, 11 Dacre, 12 Eston, 13 Galphay, 14 Heyshaw, 15 Kilnsey, 16 Kirby Wiske, 17 Malham, 18 Marston, 19 Marton, 20 Nutwith, 21 Pott, 22 Sawley, 23 Sutton, 24 Thorpe Underwood, 25 Weldrake.*

and show some evidence for slight changes of layout, excavation below the woolhouse has shown that the terracing of the hillside was no earlier than the 1150s and suggested that it was part of a planned expansion into that area from the flat ground of the valley bottom before 1160. It is perhaps not surprising that this was happening at exactly the same time as the inner court was being developed to the west of the cloister buildings, and the development of the precinct was an integral part of the development of the mature monastery under Abbots

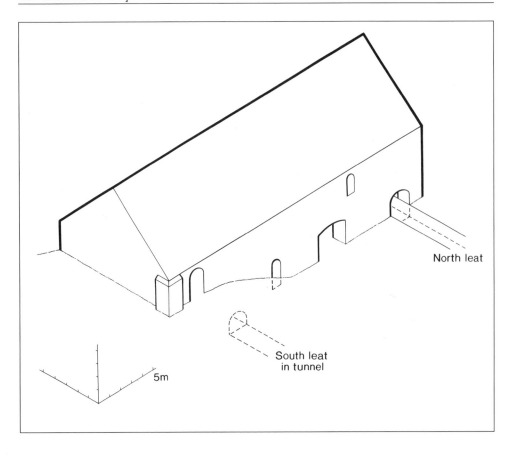

North leat

South leat
in tunnel

5m

63   The Fountains mill was rebuilt in the 1150s with a greatly increased milling capacity, a clear indication
that the needs of the community and the produce of the home estates were growing as the abbey reached
maturity.

Richard III and Robert of Pipewell. It is also significant that it was the period 1150
to 1180 that saw the principal growth of the abbey's estates, with the community
ruthlessly adding to their estates in Nidderdale and making huge inroads into
Craven where the area around Malham Tarn was brought in hand from 1174. By
1180, when the third monastery at Fountains was completed, its estates were
almost as extensive as they were when they were surveyed for the *Valor Ecclesiasticus*
of 1535 (**62**).

   It was the growth of the estates that was reflected in the two principal buildings
in the outer court in the 1150s. The mill was rebuilt (**63**), no longer a single water
wheel in a leat providing power. The old mill was partially demolished and buried
within a dam for a mill-pond which could supply a more controlled flow of water
and a second water wheel was added when a new and larger mill was built on top

of the dam doubling the milling capacity. The old mill had effectively become the basement of the new building and its growth is as much a reflection of the growth of the community in the period that followed the ending of the phase of colonisation as it is a reflection in the growth of land in cultivation. Bread and beer were the staples of monastic life, and a community of 120 monks and 400 lay brothers would have consumed approximately 5200 loaves of bread and 3640 gallons of beer a week. The amount of grain that was handled within the precinct at any time would have been substantial. On top of these figures are the unknown quantities consumed by guests and given away as charity. Associated with the development of the mill must be granaries within the precinct that handled the short-term needs of the community and on the granges that provided longer term storage.

The second building was the abbey's woolhouse (**64**), a great aisled building of five bays that was first built as the storehouse for the wool crop that was brought in from the granges for onward shipment and later extended to include the processing and cleaning of the wool. Of similar scale to the Rievaulx woolhouse of Laskill, its building in the 1150s indicates the importance of wool as a cash crop within twenty years of the foundation of the abbey and the speed with which the community had established its sheep runs on the vast areas of marginal land it was acquiring. Fountains did not simply market its own wool but acted as the agent for other monasteries, not all of them Cistercian, by the end of the twelfth century. Rebuilt and extended in the thirteenth century it became the largest building apart from the church within the precinct and was remarkably elaborate considering its function.

Fountains and Rievaulx were always exceptional, both in scale and in wealth, and there is always the risk that they were not typical of the order at large. Approximately two thirds of the Cistercian abbeys in Britain have precincts marked by earthworks which survive at least in part. In almost every case they are larger at an average of 60 acres (24ha) than the average 30 acres (12ha) for Benedictines monks or Augustinian canons. That at Bordesley has been studied intensively and though not typical of all Cistercian precinct layouts (no two are alike because they are all controlled by their geographical setting) it does contain all the elements that normally occur in a Cistercian monastery (**65**). Bordesley, too, appears to have two principal stages of development in the twelfth century. The earliest part of the site was the western half of the precinct, defined on the west and north by a substantial bank, on the east by the original course of the River Arrow (32, 37, 41, 43 on **fig. 65**), and the Red Ditch to the south. The church and cloister were placed just to the east of centre, with an area of ridge and furrow to the north which implies either cultivation or improved pasture and the complex earthworks of the inner and outer courts to the west and south. The fact that the ridge and furrow underlies the precinct boundary is not a problem, for there is no indication that the Cistercians formalised their precincts before the last years of the twelfth century, and the earliest precinct wall to be identified is that at Fountains built in the 1220s. At Croxden, the precinct wall was not built until

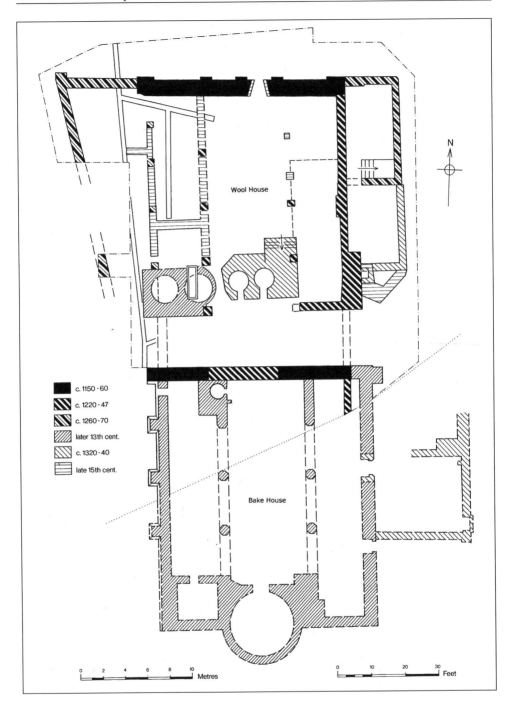

Wool House

c. 1150 - 60

c. 1220 - 47

c. 1260 - 70

later 13th cent.

c. 1320 - 40

late 15th cent.

Bake House

N

0 2 4 6 8 10
Metres

0   10   20   30
Feet

64 *The woolhouse at Fountains, excavated in the late 1970s, was built in the 1150s and rebuilt in the 1220s to process the abbey's wool crop. The scale of the building, the largest in the outer court, indicates the importance of the crop. To the south was the abbey's bake house, rebuilt in the late thirteenth century.*

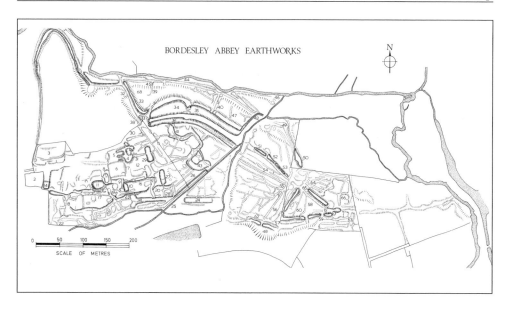

65   *The earthworks of Bordesley Abbey in the valleys of the Arrow and Red Ditch are among the finest of*
      any Cistercian abbey. 6 marks the cloister of the abbey itself, approximately 30m square (Aston).

1274, even though the gatehouse had been built in 1242. Completion of permanent building for the community seems to have been accompanied by a substantial enlargement of the precinct which required the removal of the River Arrow to the north side of its valley (44 on **fig. 65**) and the construction of a series of fish-ponds (34, 35, 36 on **fig. 65**) and a mill pond (58). This extended precinct covered some 90 acres (36ha), making Bordesley more extensive than Fountains. Water engineering is a particular feature of Cistercian precincts, and the developments at Bordesley can be paralleled at Croxden, Buildwas, Hailes, Byland, Merevale, Sawley, and Stanley. The mill at Bordesley has been excavated and identified as an iron-working mill of the late twelfth to early fourteenth centuries, with water-powered trip hammers and not the corn mill that might have been expected. That mill, in fact has been identified at (14) at the west end of the precinct on a leat taken from the Red Ditch. Why an industrial mill should be within the precinct rather than on a grange is unexplained, but Bordesley provides an undoubted example of trade and highly organised labour. This mill, like all precinct mills, was almost certainly worked by lay brothers, only going out of use with their decline.

If the precinct at Bordesley shows the scale of a Cistercian abbey, it does not show the form of the buildings that once occupied it as they have all been demolished. Many surviving buildings date from the second half of the twelfth century, showing that the mature abbey had its full suite of service buildings by then, even if enclosure within a precinct wall came later. In this, the Cistercians were not out of step with other orders, though the disposition of their buildings did not always follow the standard Benedictine layout. This was perhaps because there was a separation of function between those buildings which were the responsibility of the choir monks, and those which were the province of lay brothers, a distinction that was maintained even after the lay brethren ceased to be an important part of the community.

The area that was the preserve of the choir monks outside the cloister was the inner court, essentially a highly controlled area to which access was controlled from the inner or great gatehouse. Almost all Cistercian great gates were unique structures, a porch with a single porch and two gate-halls. They were always approached from a small outer gatehouse along a walled lane which might contain stables and the gate chapel used by the poor and women who were not allowed access to the inner court, and the first gatehall controlled access to the outer court. The second gate hall controlled access to the inner court. Occasionally, as at Kirkstall or Beaulieu, the inner gate had only one gate-hall and it was the outer gate which served the outer court, but surviving examples such as Roche (**66**), Rievaulx, Furness, Fountains, and Cleeve all have two. Great gates were always two-storey structures with a room or rooms above the gate passage and reached from it by a stair. At Cleeve it contained the gate chapel, a feature it shared with the outer gate at Whalley Abbey. The upper floor was used more often as the abbey's court house and exchequer where business with the outside world was conducted, a use for the upper floor of gatehouses shared with most other orders. Gate chapels were normally outside the inner gate, where their ruins can still be seen at Fountains and Furness, and one has been excavated in this position at Bordesley (**65**, 2). They are among the most common surviving Cistercian buildings, surviving in use as parish churches at Kirkstead, Tilty, Merevale, Thame, Rievaulx, and Hailes.

Within the inner court were the guest-houses and guest hall, the guest kitchen (which produced a richer diet including fowl and meat for visitors than could be had from the convent kitchen), stables for the guests horses, and possible as at Fountains, the lay infirmary where the better-off sick and old from outside the monastery were treated. Guest halls of the twelfth and thirteenth centuries are known at Fountains, Kirkstall, and Tintern, great aisled halls were guests lived and ate in common, and additionally Fountains had two guest houses, each with a hall and chamber at ground and first floor level, providing four separate apartments for guests of a higher social standing. Guests of the highest rank were normally given the abbot's house, and it is quite clear that the Cistercians provided their charity on a sliding scale that matched the stratification of social rank. Stables associated with guest accommodation are regularly recorded in suppression period surveys, but are only known from excavation at Kirkstall where a stable and smithy were found to the west of the guest hall. They simply have not been traced elsewhere.

All other orders of monks, and Cistercian nuns, had buildings in the inner court which served the cloister, the bake house, brew house, kiln house, and

66   *The great gate at Roche Abbey, built early in the thirteenth century at the entrance to both the inner and outer courts (author).*

granaries. At Fountains, however, the bake house (**64**) lay to the south of the woolhouse in the outer court, and was excavated by William St John Hope in the 1880s. A great aisled building of five bays with a clerestorey lighting its central aisle, it had a bread oven 5.5m in diameter at its south end, and space in the aisles for the preparation of the flour in the great bolting arks that are well recorded in sixteenth century surveys and the tables on which the dough was prepared and made up into batches. Water was piped into the building at its north end. It is the sole surviving Cistercian bake house, and it is necessary to consider it in the context of buildings recorded at Rievaulx in 1538-9 at the end of their life. Lying just to the west of the west range of the cloister was a building called the brew house by the surveyors, of eleven bays, so large it must have been a combined brew house and bakehouse. At this time, the old lay brothers' dormitory was serving as a granary, and on the other side of the brew house was the abbey's kiln house, essentially a vast grain dryer in a building eight bays long in which grain was dried for milling and barley was malted for brewing. These buildings lay in the outer court because they would originally have been worked by lay brethren. On their demise they were operated by servants, and so lay outside the area of the inner court.

Other buildings known to lie in the Cistercian outer court were tanneries. At Fountains it lay somewhere between the mill and the woolhouse, though its site

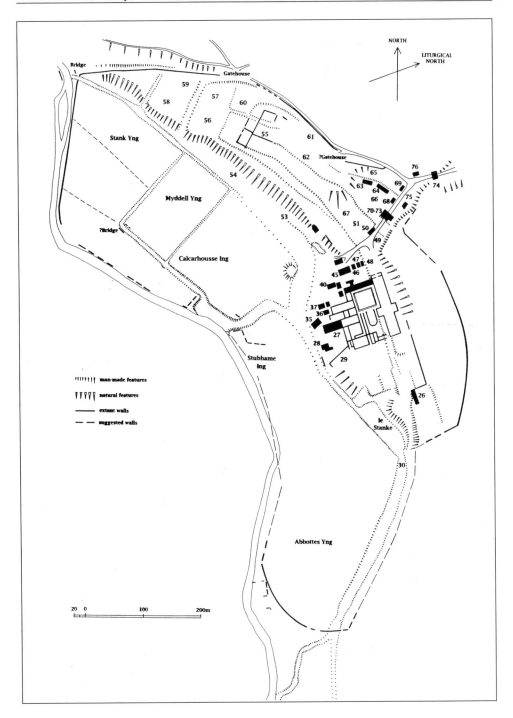

67   *The precinct of Rievaulx Abbey reconstructed from its earthworks, standing ruins, and the evidence of sixteenth-century documents (Atkins and Coppack).*

has never been identified with any certainty. At Rievaulx, perhaps exceptionally, the tannery occupied the south end of the monks' east range, abandoned and partly demolished in the late fourteenth century. In the sixteenth century, the tannery or bark house comprised a whole series of buildings: the tannery itself with its tanning vats, and a small yard to its south, and around this the mill for grinding up the oak bark used in tanning, a lime kiln, the bark store, a small barn, and the house of the tanner himself. It was obviously a substantial undertaking. Rievaulx, too, gives some indication of what the small buildings in the outer court at Fountains must have been. There were the houses of the convent plumber and blacksmith, the house of the porter at the parlour door, the common stable, the well house, houses for some 13 court servants and pensioners of the abbey, workshops, mills, orchards, and small closes of pasture (**67**). When Rievaulx was suppressed in 1538 the community employed 102 servants, most of whom worked within the precinct and the home granges of Griff and Newlathes, supporting an abbot and twenty-one monks.

Granges and land holdings

Early Cistercian legislation required that granges or estate centres should be no more than a day's ride from the abbey so that the community could keep them under adequate control, and the first granges established by Fountains for instance (**57**) indicate that this was initially the case. However, it was not always possible to acquire land in the vicinity of the monastery, and from the middle years of the twelfth century it was common to find granges at some distance from the house. Staying with the example of Fountains, it is possible to see a network of granges set out to exploit a mixed economy across a wide swathe of north and east Yorkshire, exploiting both upland and lowland economies from the Derwent in the east to Lancaster and Cumberland in the north-west (**62**). To the north of the abbey were the home granges of Swanley, Galphay, and Sutton, to the south-west Warsill, and to the south Morker or Herleshowe, Haddockstanes, and Cayton. Beyond these, further granges were set in the lower dales that provided access into the Pennines. Lower Wensleydale was managed from Sleningford, while the upper reaches were administered from Nutwith and Aldburgh. Pott grange lay on the flank of Colsterdale, and Bramley at the head waters of the river Laver. Lower Nidderdale was served by Dacre, with its lodges of Brimham, Bewerley, and Heyshaw; and the upper dale by Bouthwaite and its lodge of Lofthouse. Huge tracts of land on the east side of the dale at Dallow Moor and Fountains Earth Moor were administered from Bouthwaite. Kilnsey served upper Wharfedale and Arncliffe served Littondale; serviced by the lodges of Foxup, Cosh, Upper and Lower Heseldon and Fornagill, tucked into the side valleys that provided access to the high moors. Fountains Fell, on the south side of Pen-y-Ghent is named from the abbey's sheep runs there. Malham and the twin granges of Bordley lay in Craven, above Airedale, and Arnfold managed lands in Ribblesdale. To the north-

68   *The Fountains grange at Kilnsey in upper Wharfedale is a typical upland grange with substantial buildings and closes (RCHM(E)).*

69   *The gatehouse range at Kilnsea grange, rebuilt in the fourteenth century (Roebuck).*

70   *The great late thirteenth-century barn on the Beaulieu Abbey grange of Great Coxwell is the most
      important Cistercian barn in Britain (Kinder).*

east of the abbey, the route into Teesdale was marked by a progression of granges at Kirby Wiske, Cowton, Busby, and Eston; and to the south-east a similar placing of granges at Marton, Thorpe Underwood, and Marston led to the grange of Wheldrake on the river Derwent. Only two granges, that of Allerdale in Cumberland and the grange of Bradley near Huddersfield lay outside this network.

Granges were effectively staging-posts one to another, connected by droveways like Mastiles Lane that led from Kilnsey onto Malham Moor which can still be traced in the Pennines, often with wayleaves to pass over land that Fountains itself did not control. The focus of the whole estate was the abbey itself, and it is clear from surviving charters and leases that Fountains targeted specific areas, traded land it could not manage efficiently for land it could, and sought as broad based an economy as it could, virtually completing its network of granges by the early years of the thirteenth century. The development of the estate in fact exactly mirrors the development of the abbey itself.

The granges were the preserve of the lay brothers from the twelfth to the late thirteenth century, and they appear to have been as highly organised as the abbey precinct with substantial buildings at their core. Fountains' grange at Kilnsey is typical of many upland granges (**68**), with walled closes containing a whole series of buildings, some domestic including a chapel, a dormitory, and a refectory, some for animals and agricultural storage, and others for industry. The degree of organisation is apparent from the fact that the nearby grange of Malham had a piped water supply before 1190-1210. The lay brethren enjoyed much the same facilities as they did in the monastery itself. Surrounding the grange buildings were walled stock enclosures and droveways, and the satellite lodges that provided accommodation for a smaller number of men. Few grange buildings survive today, either because lowland granges have been rebuilt and the upland granges, always on marginal land, were abandoned, in some cases before the suppression. There are, however, some important survivors, for instance a barn at the Fountains grange of Sutton, only recently identified, the gatehouse range at Kilnsey (**69**), chapels at the Jervaulx grange of Thrintoft and the Fountains granges of Morker and Bouthwaite. Barns are the greatest survivors, and some two dozen have been identified, either as standing buildings, ruins, or from documents. They come in three sizes, large more than 45m long, medium more than 15m long, and small. The smallest, at Vaudey's grange of Sewstern in Leicestershire was tiny, only 4.5m by 2.9m, and probably had a specialist use. Perhaps more typical was the Neath barn at Marcross in Glamorgan, 26m long, or the Flaxley barn at Dymock in Somerset, 33m long. Large barns survive at Buckland, and at Coggeshall on home granges, and on the Calcot grange of Kingswood Abbey in Gloucestershire. By far the most important is the great barn of Beaulieu Abbey on its grange of Great Coxwell in Oxfordshire (**70**), built in the late thirteenth century. Every grange would have had at least one barn and the scale of the Great Coxwell barn is not exceptional. A second and even larger barn survives as a ruin on the Beaulieu grange of St Leonards in Hampshire, and a third, again of like size, existed at Wyke, the grange on the site of the initial foundation of Faringdon (**71**), demolished in the seventeenth century. Wyke can be taken as a typical lowland grange with a mixed economy, its buildings modified and replaced over some three centuries, and now only known from aerial photography. Many others can be identified from their earthworks and standing ruins. Neath Abbey's grange of Monknash in South Glamorgan (**72**) with its surviving dovecote and ruinous barn matches Wyke both in scale and layout, and the same features can be seen on many of Bordesley's granges which have recently been surveyed by Mick Aston and Grenville Astill. A feature of the Bordesley granges was the provision of water mills, with waterworks every bit as complex as those within the abbey precinct. At their grange of Lye in Worcestershire, the mill was given in 1180 by one William Baker in exchange for an annuity of 12 quarters of wheat and 12 of rye, and thus was not a monastic creation.

The Cistercian statutes forbade the possession of mills that might be used as a source of revenue, but this was easier said than done. In many areas, the White Monks were occupying a landscape which was already well developed and many of the mills they were to acquire already existed. Bordesley was given the mill of Bidford on its foundation as a useful source of cash revenue in its first years, and Louth Park was similarly provided for by Bishop Alexander. Others were built as granges were developed, as for instance on the Fountains grange of Bradley, where the abbey had great difficulty in building a mill on the river Calder to serve its

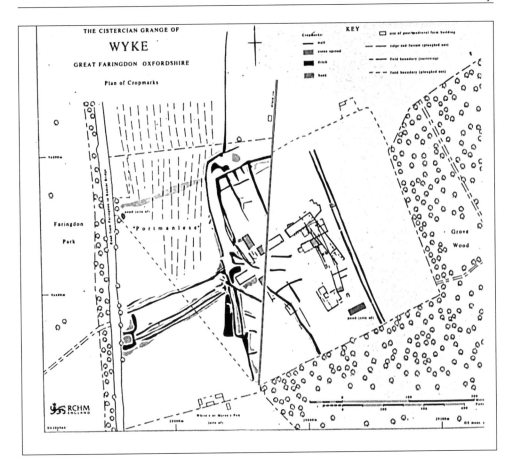

71   *Wyke Grange at Faringdon, plotted from the evidence of aerial photography, shows the layout of a*
typical lowland grange not obscured by post-medieval development (RCHME)

grange because of the prioress of Kirklees' mill upstream (**74**). For once the might
of Fountains could not overawe a smaller community, and the abbey had to build
its mill on the river Colne that ran through the grange lands. Water power was
always preferred to wind power as it was more reliable and capable of exploitation
on an industrial scale. Some granges, however, did have wind-mills, as a fine
fourteenth-century carving of a post-mill from Rievaulx demonstrates (**73**).
Whalley Abbey had a post-mill at Ince in Cheshire by about 1230, and Thame had
one on its grange at Otley in about 1237. Beaulieu's accounts for 1269-70 refer to
two newly built wind-mills at Rydon and Great Coxwell. Abbot Adam of Skyrne
of Meaux built a wind-mill at his grange of Wawne before 1339, and a later abbot
moved a wind-mill from Beeford to Dringhoe to replace a decayed water mill. By
the late Middle ages, wind-power had overtaken water power in the monastic
economy.

72   *Monknash Grange, the finest surviving Cistercian grange in Wales, survives as clear earthworks with the ruins of a dovecote and barn. Its other buildings can be seen in plan, almost exactly copying the layout of Wyke (Cambridge University Collection).*

73 A late fourteenth-century post-mill carved on a section of cornice moulding from Rievaulx Abbey which also depicts a flock of sheep and other agricultural scenes from the abbey's estates.

Industrial granges were common and were developed from the third quarter of the twelfth century. Boxley, Byland, Flaxley, Fountains, Furness, Kirkstall, Rievaulx, and Stanley all worked iron on their estates, and Rievaulx and Merevale also had ironworks within their precincts in the early sixteenth century. Boxley's ironworks of Chingley in the Weald has been excavated, but its was small in comparison to the complex that Fountains had established at Bradley (**74**) or Rievaulx had developed at Fawether. Bradley was a holding of some 4400 acres (1780ha) assembled by 1193 from a series of small grants in the townships of Huddersfield and Kirkheaton, the extents of which can be recovered from charter evidence. Almost certainly, the abbey had targeted the area because of its industrial potential, and as individual holdings were acquired, wayleaves were negotiated between them in a way which suggests the community had a master-plan for the area that would give them access to iron ore, timber for smelting, and water to drive their machinery. The site of the principal ironworks of Smytheclough (I on **74**) can be identified from its dam, watercourses, and heaps of iron slag and hammer scale, one of the earliest industrial ironworks in Britain which is known to have been operating by 1194. Iron was not the only industry practised at Bradley. Pottery kilns at Upper Heaton (P on **74**) served Fountains properties in south and west Yorkshire, and were rarely traded off the estate. Fountains had a second pottery site at Sutton, where the Winksley kilns served the abbey and properties to the north and east in the late twelfth and thirteenth centuries, though again the pottery was not widely traded to non-monastic sites. There are

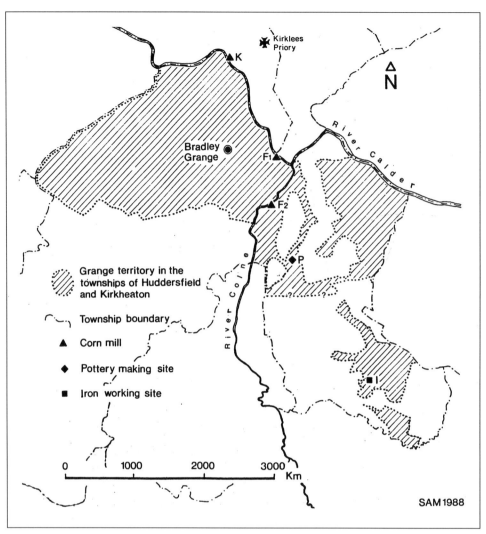

74   *Reconstructed from charter evidence, the lands of Bradley Grange were extensive and supported industry as well as agriculture (Moorhouse).*

indications that the family network functioned across Cistercian estates, for Fountains daughter-house of Meaux in Holderness had a major tile kiln at its North Grange which produced mosaic tiles not only for Meaux but for Fountains and Sawley as well, and possibly for other members of the family.

The later medieval economy

The White Monks' economy was fully developed by the early years of the thirteenth century, and they had begun to make substantial profits from their estates. Their principal cash-crop was wool, and the Cistercians were beginning to establish trading connections with the international wool markets of Flanders and Italy, securing royal licences for export. A list from the 1260s identifies 102 monastic houses trading in wool with Flanders, of which many were Cistercian. The house which topped the list was the Cistercian abbey of Neath. A generation later, the *Pratica della Mercatura* of Francesco Balducci Pegolotti lists 55 Cistercian monasteries trading with Flemish and Italian merchants out of a total of 65 abbeys and priories. Fountains was the chief exporter with 76 sacks of wool for export, Rievaulx was second with 60 sacks, and Jervaulx equalled the great Benedictine cathedral priory of Christchurch in Canterbury with 50 sacks. A sack of wool contained the fleeces of some 220 sheep, allowing a rough calculation to be made of the size of flocks. However, it is likely that the greater monasteries were also acting as agents for smaller ones, and Fountains maintained its own ship to transport wool from York to Boston, and had a woolhouse there, an indication of the scale of its involvement in the wool trade.

Over-specialisation had its problems, and the Cistercians were tempted to speculate on the basis of their cash revenues, selling their crops several years in advance. This would not have been a problem if production could be guaranteed. The late thirteenth century, however, brought a period of worsening climate, coupled with a serious outbreak of sheep-scab or murrain in the 1280s. Rievaulx was an early casualty, its wool crop falling well short of what had already been sold, and was forced to buy in wool to make up the deficit. By 1279, the abbey was sufficiently in debt for the king to appoint Alexander of Kirketon to sort the situation out. In 1288, the abbey was again taken into royal protection, with the Bishop of Durham appointed as keeper, as the debt increased. How serious the debt was is not recorded, but Fountains trading on a greater scale, saw its indebtedness rise from £900 in 1274 to a catastrophic £6373 in 1291. In 1276, Abbot Peter Ayling had even pledged his abbey as security for a four year contract for his wool. Meaux Abbey was in even worse trouble, with a debt of £3678 in 1280, of which some £2500 was owed to wool merchants and money lenders. It was not simply the great houses that suffered, only that their levels of distress are better documented, and it is not without significance that this economic downturn matches the beginning of the decline in the numbers of lay brethren. It had become apparent that one of the ways of dealing with indebtedness was to lease estates for cash.

From the late twelfth century, the lay brothers who had created the wealth of the White Monks began to become a problem. Resenting their second class status and the harsh conditions in which they often worked, they began to rebel. Discontent was particularly apparent on distant granges where the control of the abbot was less easily maintained. The General Chapter's response was to ban beer drinking in an attempt to reduce the growing problem of drunkenness, and in 1208 to allow the leasing out of distant granges. This gradually weakened the Cistercian's reliance on lay brothers, and by the late thirteenth century it was already established that land which senior monks felt was 'less useful' could also be leased out.

The late thirteenth century saw damage to the economies of many of the Welsh houses in Edward I's wars, a problem too for the Scots, and for the northern English houses after the English defeat at Bannockburn in 1314. It was not only the depredations of armies on the march, burning granges and seizing food, but the king also required abbots as landowners owing him service to provide levies for the royal army together with food and transport. Edward II required the abbot of Sawley to provide such assistance in 1318, just at the time his estates were in turmoil because of Scots incursions, and Abbot Walter Coxwold of Fountains had to supply troops in 1318, 1321, and 1322. Fountains and Rievaulx suffered badly, with granges destroyed and the Scots army routing Edward II at the Battle of Byland on Shaws Moor almost within site of Rievaulx. Rievaulx itself was plundered. Recovery called for desperate measures, and Fountains began to run its surviving granges with hired labour under a bailiff, and rented out its damaged ones in 1336. The final break with Cistercian tradition came in 1363, when Abbot Robert Monkton converted the surviving granges into vills, reversing the earlier policy of depopulation and using peasant labour to farm them. At the Fountains grange of Cowton, the great twelfth century barns were swept away, to be replaced by smaller buildings of manorial scale. In this, Fountains was only doing what other houses were also forced to do as the supply of lay brothers effectively dried up. There was, however, a difference in the way Fountains chose to manage its estate that might not be typical, for new tenants were not allowed to farm the land as they chose and the abbey supplied their buildings and stock. If a cow died, for instance, the tenant would be given a replacement on production of the dead cow's hide at the abbey's tannery. The tenant was more of a manager, wearing the abbot's uniform or livery, and owed service in a feudal manner to the abbey, showing that the estate was still managed in a centralised way, its economic base still dictated by the convent.

Within the precinct, changes were also occurring. Redundant building, like the woolhouse at Fountains, were first converted to other uses, and finally demolished when they were no longer of any use or worth maintaining, precisely what had happened to cloister ranges that were to large for their reduced communities. Hired labour, again under a bailiff, replaced the lay brothers, and the effect of this can be seen with particular clarity at Rievaulx. Houses for lay men and their families appeared in the outer court, bringing women into the precinct for the first time. The wife of the keeper of the western gates at Fountains was employed as the convent's laundress, for instance, and female servants were not uncommon, requiring a greater separation of the outer court from the rest of the establishment. At Rievaulx, some seven houses with their own crofts were built between the inner and outer gate houses for senior servants of the abbey and their families, in addition to the swine house with its house for the husband and wife team who managed it. The mills and tannery within the precinct were let out to laymen, and workshops and houses were provided for the abbey's smith and plumber, bringing lay tradesmen into the abbey. In time, some of these properties came to be occupied by pensioned servants of the abbey from granges which were still farmed in hand, and when the abbey was suppressed, it was these which became the village that replaced it. Effectively, the abbey's economy was to continue under lay management to the present day.

6 The end of Cistercian monasteries in Britain

The later Middle Ages was a period of decline for the traditional orders of monks, including the Cistercians, as the urban friars and the eremitic Carthusians attracted some of the most able to the cloister. Great monasteries built for hundreds of monks and lay brothers no longer attracted sufficient religious to fill them, and declining incomes from largely tenanted estates (coupled with a raised standard of living expected by the religious) meant that many houses were no longer able to sustain large communities. In 1381-2, Rievaulx had only fifteen choir monks, and many monasteries had even less. In spite of reduced numbers and a distinct lack of new patronage, the White Monks continued to develop, and by the middle years of the fifteenth century, a small renaissance is apparent in many houses of the order. It was not only the wealthy houses like Rievaulx, Fountains, and Furness which experienced this, though they are the houses which show it most clearly in their surviving buildings. Cleeve, a relatively poor house in comparison had in Abbots David Juyner (1435-87) and William Dovell (1510-36) two capable administrators and builders who had begun the task of bringing their abbey up to date (**col. pl. 21**).

Traces of late medieval development are often slight, but some indications do remain. At Bordesley, Combe, Croxden, Forde, Hailes, Kirkstall, St Mary Graces in London, and Strata Florida new glazed cloister alleys were built from the late fifteenth century, and it is likely that this was part of a wider reorganisation of the monastery with the partitioning of dormitories, the provision of a meat refectory, and a meat kitchen, all suggestive of a well-ordered and thriving community. Churches, too, were being repaired, re-windowed, and redecorated from the mid-fifteenth century. William Angel, last abbot of Sawtry, reglazed the west window, and borrowed £20 for timber for the rebuilding of his church. Fountains and Jervaulx (**col. pl. 13**) had new screen-work and stalls of the finest quality, and Abbot Leyshon Thomas of Neath presided over a church with 'crystal windows of every colour' and a 'gold-adorned choir, the nave, the gilded tabernacle work, the pinnacles ... a vast and lofty roof ... like the sparkling heavens on high'. Clearly, the church here had been restored, though it would have been unrecognisable to the first monks who settled there and who shunned coloured glass, gilding, and carving that distracted them from prayer and meditation.

Not all was well in the later Middle Ages, however, and there were houses which through bad management had fallen into debt. With debt came the inevitable downturn in religious life and lack of maintenance of buildings. Rievaulx, a well-managed house to the end, was clearly in a bad state of maintenance, and when the house was suppressed, the spire and part of the crossing tower was already lying where it had fallen into the south transept. Elsewhere, the picture was worse. At Vaudey in the early sixteenth century, Abbot William Style claimed 'the body of my church fell down and the rebuilding cost me £100' and at Garendon in 1535, it was claimed that the 'large old monastery was partly ruinous'. At Strata Florida, both the infirmary and refectory were ruinous in the early sixteenth century. Strata Marcella, heavily in debt by the 1530s, was also ruinous, with its community reduced to only two or three monks. Saddell Abbey had actually ceased to exist before 1507 when King James IV of Scotland sought to transfer its estates to the cathedral of Argyll and Lismore, claiming that there had been no monastic life within living memory.

The general state of the monastic church in the early sixteenth century was far from good in many instances. In this, the White Monks were no worse than any other monks with the exception of the Carthusians, and they had less to offer in a rapidly secularised world. Many of their communities were down to ten monks or less, and their lands were jealously regarded by their neighbours and their tenants at a time when there was little land on the open market to satisfy a growing middle class. The monks themselves were seen as a non-productive element of society, taking from others but putting very little back. The early seeds of Protestantism had been sown in the late fourteenth century by John Wycliffe and his followers, and more than a hint of suspicion remained that the general populace was being taken advantage of by the church, and by the monastic church in particular. Cardinal Wolsey had begun a reform of the monastic church in the 1520s, when he had suppressed no fewer than 29 houses including the priory of St Frideswide in Oxford with Papal authority, using their lands and buildings to endow educational rather than religious institutions. In this, he was assisted by his secretary, Thomas Cromwell. In England and Wales, it was the refusal of the Pope to grant Henry VIII a divorce that led indirectly to the suppression of all monasteries in the kingdom between 1536 and 1540. With popular support, because the English generally had little time for foreign interference in the church, he broke with Rome.

Henry VIII was recognised by the English clergy as 'Supreme Head of the Church in England ... in so far as the law of Christ allows', a position which was finally confirmed by Parliament in 1534. As Head of the Church, Henry took up again the movement for reform which had been started by Wolsey, but was motivated as much by the need to bring the English church under his own control as he was with the need to remove the abuses which were bringing it into disrepute. The White Monks were exempt by Papal authority from episcopal visitation which in other orders ensured that monastic discipline was well kept, though they had their own system of visitation which was in many ways more efficient. However, some of the Cistercian visitors were foreigners, not answerable to the English Crown and therefore not acceptable to the king. Henry replaced them with a commission of five Cistercian abbots headed by William Thirsk of Fountains to act on his behalf in April 1532. This new commission, very much aware of Cistercian tradition, set about its task at Vaudey, where its members were taken to task for their zeal in correcting faults. The following year they were sent to investigate the alleged poisoning of the abbot of Holmcultram, and then to investigate and depose Abbot Edward Kirby of Rievaulx. This last visitation was a nasty piece of work, for Thomas Cromwell, now the king's secretary, wished to impose his own candidate, Rowland Blyton, abbot of Rufford, in place of the conservative Abbot Kirby. William Thirsk believed that he did not have the authority to depose another abbot without recourse to normal Cistercian disciplinary machinery, and could find little reason to find fault with Kirby. Cromwell's reply was that Abbot Thirsk cared too much for 'the rules of his religion' to be an effective instrument of the king's chief minister. Ultimately, though Thirsk was able to absent himself on the excuse of more pressing royal business, Kirby was deposed, and Thirsk followed him three years later.

It soon became clear that the government would take the monasteries in hand, and the beginning of the end came in the spring and summer of 1535 when the king ordered a valuation of the church, the *Valor Ecclesiasticus*. Commissioners were sent to every religious house to collect information on the taxable income and exempt expenditure, providing the government for the first time with a reliable indication of the net wealth of the monastic church and the extent of its land-holdings. While the primary purpose of the *Valor* was to assess taxation, it had a second use in indicating which monasteries were barely viable. In parallel with this survey, other commissioners were appointed to assess the condition of religious life by Thomas Cromwell, now the king's Vicar General. Unlike the commissioners for the *Valor* who were the usual agents for the Crown in the shires and who reflected local opinion, those sent out to survey religious life were Cromwell's own men working to his directives. They were required to find fault and show monastic communities in the worst possible light. Not only were they to identify faults, mainly sexual, they were to identify which monks wished to leave the cloister. This they achieved in a remarkably short period, though a comparison of their findings with contemporary bishops' visitations suggests that their report, the *Compendium Compertorum* or Black Book, was largely a work of fiction. In 1536, an bill was placed before Parliament for the suppression of all religious houses with a taxable income of less than £200 where 'manifest sin, vicious and abominable living' was daily practised. The displaced monks were either to be transferred to wealthier 'divers and great solemn monasteries of this realm wherein, thanks be to God, religion is right well kept and observed', or to take 'capacities' and leave the cloister but not their vows.

Thirty-three Cistercian monasteries were caught in the net of the first Act of Suppression, of which the most important were Waverley with an income of £174 and Tintern with an income of £192. Others included Cleeve, Louth Park, Rufford, Stanley, and Stoneleigh. In the spring and summer of 1536, 26 monasteries were closed, and quite remarkably, the monks of Sibton, seeing how the future looked, sold their monastery and its lands to Thomas Howard, Duke of Norfolk and suppressed themselves. The Welsh houses of Aberconwy and Basingwerk struggled on until March 1537 when they too were suppressed. Five small monasteries, Bindon, Croxden, Neath, Strata Florida, and Whitland, purchased a continuance from the government, but at an immense cost. Bindon, with an income of £147 paid £300 for the privilege of not being suppressed immediately. The suppressed monasteries passed to the crown as Head of the Church, and a new body, the Court of the Augmentations of the Revenues of the King's Crown was set up to administer the seized property.

Commissioners were appointed to oversee the suppression of the smaller monasteries, again local men, but this time stiffened by support of clerks from the Court of Augmentations. They were to take the surrender of the community, to account for its possessions, to survey its buildings and lands, and to sell any moveables and stock by auction. In the early days, before suppression was fully organised, things could go badly wrong with the local populace taking away what they chose before the commissioners could arrange a sale. It is fairly clear that the suppression of the minor houses was not worked out particularly well before the process began, but then the government was not expecting very great returns. The poorest house was Grace Dieu in Wales with an income of barely £19 and the average value of the small houses was only £125. Even so, the contents of the smaller houses had some value. At Sawtry, the church plate which was reserved for the Crown amounted to 306 ounces of silver, of which 134 had been pawned by the convent for £10. In the church, the auction of its fittings, the brass lectern and candle sticks, the lamps and censers, two pairs of organs, an old clock, the sacring bells, cruets, and altar cloths fetched £11 15s 5d (£11.77). The church had a lead roof and four bells, all of high value. Within the precinct were 29 cattle, 14 draught oxen, 7 mares, 2 geldings, 2 horses, 4 fillies, a horse colt and yearling, 6 cart horses, 17 steers and heifers, 15 yearlings, 218 sheep, 72 pigs, and two saddle horses all of which sold for £78. Including the furnishings of the cloister ranges and the contents of the grange barns, the contents of a relatively poor Cistercian monastery could amount to several hundred pounds before the building materials and land were realised.

The lands were initially managed by the Court of Augmentations who paid off the servants, and then began to lease or sell the houses and their estates. Initially, the government had no wish to damage valuable property which could easily be converted into great houses for new landowners. Roofs were stripped of their lead, and bells were removed, leaded windows removed for their scrap value. At Margam, the site complete with its stripped buildings was entrusted on the king's behalf to Sir Rice Mansell who was to lease both the abbey and much of its estates between 1540 and 1557. The nave of the church was in parochial use no later than 1542, and Mansell began the construction of a house for himself within the south and east ranges of the cloister by 1552. This was the fate of many of the smaller monasteries. At Buildwas, the abbot's house needed little conversion to provide a house for the new owner, and the church survived because it was capable of re-use as a barn. Sir William Paulet converted the church at Netley into his house, retaining all but the refectory . At Tilty, the site was acquired by Margaret Countess of Dorset, who had been resident for some years in the guest house, effectively confirming her occupation. Only at Louth Park, Tintern, Vaudey, Strata Marcella, Stanley, and Basingwerk were the sites deserted. Stone from Basingwerk went to repair Holt castle, Quarr's buildings were largely demolished within four years to build forts at East and West Cowes, and many of the White Monks' bells were recast as cannon for the defence of the realm. Little went to waste and the smaller monasteries were soon to disappear.

The events of 1536 coupled with more general worries about government policy led to two revolts in England, The Pilgrimage of Grace and the Lincolnshire Rising. The first, which began in Yorkshire, was a reaction against the government and its programme of reform, against rising inflation, and particularly against the actions of Cromwell, Archbishop Thomas Cranmer, and Sir Richard Rich, first Chancellor of the Court of Augmentation. Marching behind a banner of the Five Wounds of Christ, the rebels coerced the presidents of surviving monasteries to support them, and sought to put back displaced monks, hoping to reverse the process of suppression that they thought was ill advised. While dispossessed monks might have supported the rebels, the greater monasteries by and large kept their distance. Abbot Adam Sedbar of Jervaulx was pursued until he agreed to support the rebels, who had threatened to burn his monastery if he did not, though his support was hardly encouraging, and he went home after four days. Ex-abbot Thirsk of Fountains who was resident at Jervaulx also found himself caught up in the revolt, and the two men were to be executed later as traitors for their minor involvement. More involved were the monks of Sawley who were put back into their house by the rebels, and who were to be removed again by the earl of Derby who was instructed by the king himself to 'take the said abbot and monks with their assistants forth with violence and without any manner of delay, in their monks' apparel, [and] cause them to be hanged up as most arrant traitors and movers of insurrection accordingly'. They were, the king said, to be hanged from the steeple of the monastery, though it did not have one. In fact, a general amnesty intervened in October 1536 and the Sawley monks were to remain in residence until February 1537 when the revolt was rekindled, and the abbot was taken and tried. He may have died naturally before he could be executed. His monks simply disappear from history, and excavation has not revealed a trace of their re-occupation (**col. pl. 20**).

The abbot and convent of neighbouring Whalley were also implicated, and the abbot of Whalley, John Paslew, was executed with a Sawley monk he had sheltered in March 1537. The Lincolnshire Rising caught up the abbot of Kirkstead who only joined the rebels under duress, but was executed as a traitor none the less. Treason provided the Crown with an excuse to seize wealthy monasteries as the possessions of their presidents, and Jervaulx and Kirkstead fell to the King as a result. The monks of Whalley, though their house was not to be seized, decided that it would be wisest to surrender it to the king before more serious charges were investigated. In this way, three wealthy Cistercian abbeys passed to the king directly. The roof leads alone of Jervaulx and Kirkstead were valued at £1000, and both houses had valuable estates. The crown, which had seen little profit out of the smaller houses, could suddenly see what potential existed for exploiting the larger ones. The forfeit houses were not broken up by the Court of Augmentations but by the much more experienced Exchequer, and there was not the haste that marked the first suppressions. When Sir Arthur Darcy had been granted Sawley in 1536, its lands came unsurveyed. In comparison, it took almost five months to survey the Jervaulx estates and the first formal leases were not made until the beginning of 1538. Mistakes were made, for late in the year the lead roofs were cast down into ingots of half a ton which could not be removed from the site until the following spring because the season was wet and the roads were foul. The bells had been offered for sale locally, but there were no takers. They too had to wait for the spring before the could be transported to London. Lack of speed actually enhanced the crown's profits.

The suppression of the smaller houses had also stimulated the land market, and both Cromwell and the Court of Augmentations were coming under pressure from would-be land owners to make more monastic land available. Whalley Abbey had shown the way, voluntarily surrendering to the king's mercy. Furness, also marginally involved with the Pilgrimage of Grace followed suit, and surrendered itself in 1537. The process of voluntary surrender was one which appealed to Cromwell and the king because it did nor require fresh legislation. It also marked a change in approach, for the desire to reform was replaced with a policy to remove all monasteries which was developed in the second half of 1537. Suppression was to be by agreement, and it was going to be a slow process. Warden was the first of the greater Cistercian abbeys to be suppressed at the end of 1537 by this method, the suppression commissioners taking advantage of discord within the community to persuade them to surrender. Monks were no longer allowed to transfer to other houses, but would all receive pensions if they went without trouble. The level of pensions was left to the suppression commissioners, and in some cases they were very generous with abbots, in whose interest it was to convince their communities to resign. By this means, a further 31 houses were surrendered between January 1538 and 24 December 1539 when the last Cistercian community in England and Wales was disbanded at Hailes.

Two sites have produced good descriptions of the process of spoliation after the suppression commissioners had pensioned off the monks. At Roche, the last abbot, Henry Cundal, was granted an annual pension of £33, allowed to keep his books and to take a quarter of the abbey's plate, his household stuff, and the house's cattle. The Commissioners then began the casting down of the roof leads, using screens and the choir stalls from the church to fuel the furnaces. Even the tiles and paving were torn up and removed. Before an auction could be arranged, however, the local populace descended on the site, and 'all things of price were either spoiled, carped away [stolen], or defaced to the uttermost ... it seemeth that every person bent himself to filch and spoil what he could'. So commented Michael Sherbrook, whose father had been present at the stripping of the site and had bought timber from the church, even though he had always thought well of the monks. He was not, however, going to miss the chance to profit as others would undoubtedly gain from the wreckage. A similar occurrence is recorded at Pipewell, where the site was disposed of entire but for its lead roofs and bells to Sir William Parr, but before he could begin its stripping the local population helped themselves.

At Rievaulx, however, a more efficient and secure process was employed. The site of the abbey and its home granges were leased to Sir Thomas Manners, now first earl of Rutland, the patron of the monastery, immediately the house was dissolved on 3 December 1538. Rutland was responsible for casting down the king's lead, but was also required to deface the buildings in such a way as to make it impossible for the monks to return. He could then exploit the site in whatever way he chose. What is remarkable is the survival of a number of documents written by Rutland's steward Rauf Bawde which document the whole process of demolition. The first thing which is apparent in these documents is that not all of the roof leads were reserved for the king, and the roofs of the west range and abbot's house were specifically granted to Rutland. These were on buildings which were re-useable, and though the roof on the west range was later sold, the roof remained on the abbot's house, suggesting it was to be retained as a useful mansion for a tenant. Initially, the king's lead remained in place, but was soon to be cast down using the roof of the cloister alleys as fuel. The king's lead was then cast into pigs or 'sowes' of a half fother (half a short ton) which were stored in the nave. Four of these were recovered in 1920, buried when the nave itself collapsed (**75**). Contracts were then made for the sale of fittings, even the nails of the roof boards were to be recovered, and window glass was to be sorted into three kinds – the best to be kept, the second best to be sold, and the third quality broken up for scrap. Even the lead dowels that held the nook shafts in the presbytery windows were sold unseen. To make the monks' own buildings unusable, the piers of the chapter house and day room were partly cut through (**col. pl. 22**), ropes were attached and the piers pulled out to fell the vaults. A skeleton found below a fallen pier in the chapter house was that of an unlucky workman who failed to get out before the building collapsed.

What happened at Rievaulx happened on most other sites. The stone was hardly worth recovering and the buildings were simply abandoned to be informally quarried for local building work and for field walls (**col. pl. 23**). Where good building stone was not readily available, as in Lincolnshire, the destruction was almost total. Sites like Kirkstead and Revesby are marked not by the presence of mounds over buried walls, but by the upcast waste from robber trenches that have removed even the foundations in places. In some cases, the stone was required for the king's works; Meaux was demolished to provide the stone core of a new brick

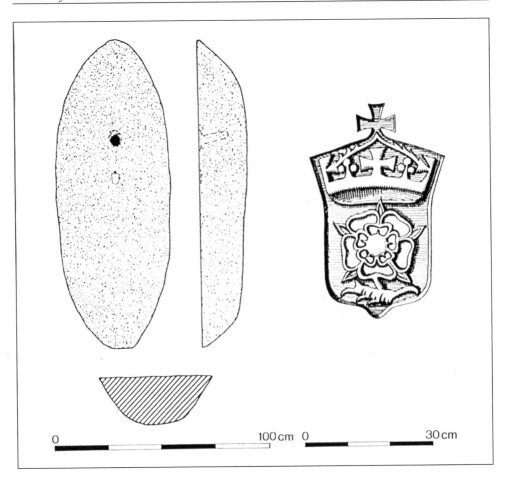

75   *Four lead 'Sows' from the stripping of Rievaulx were preserved by a falll of masonry. Each was marked with the royal stamp to identify them as the King's property.*

citadel and curtain wall that Henry VIII was raising on the east side of his town and port of Hull. It is perhaps ironic that Meaux Abbey was demolished to provide defences for a place called Wyke that the Abbot of Meaux had sold to Edward I towards the close of the thirteenth century.

Elsewhere, Cistercian monasteries became houses. At Hailes, the abbot's house in the west range was extended to become a fine mansion, with the cloister a walled garden, though the church was completely levelled. The same happened at Combe, where Aidan Nesfield's rebuilding of a post-suppression house can still be seen, and at Stoneleigh, where the east cloister range can still be identified within an eighteenth century house, or at Thame where the precinct became the park of a post-medieval house that contains substantial elements of the Cistercian monastery. The location of Cistercian abbeys away from centres of population made their re-use difficult. The most remarkable site is Dore, where the monks' church was acquired for parish use by the Scudamores, and substantially restored in the seventeenth century. Though the nave was demolished, the transepts and presbytery remain the finest surviving Cistercian building in Britain. The Golden Valley had barely sufficient people to maintain the church in the seventeenth century; that it should survived today is quite remarkable.

The reformation came to Scotland slightly later than it did in England and Wales, and the end of Cistercian monasteries was a much slower and less well documented process. As in England, Cistercian monasteries were showing signs of falling standards. In 1530, King James V arranged with the General Chapter of the order for Deer and Coupar Angus to be visited, intending that they be reformed. He did not, however, like the advice that was proffered, feeling that it did not sufficiently allow for Scottish conditions. One of those conditions was the increasing prevalence of monasteries headed not by abbots but by Commendators, laymen who were appointed by the Crown to the headships of religious houses. The first commendators had at least been priests, but later appointees were royal bastards and placemen whose only interest was to exploit the income of the house at the expense of the religious.

Culross had been in the hands of a commendator since 1511 and Dundrennan since 1523. At Kinloss, the reforming abbot Thomas Crystal, who had brought his abbey to good financial and spiritual order, resigned in 1528 in favour of Robert Reid, a secular priest. In 1529, however, Reid was professed a Cistercian monk and remained therefore a proper abbot rather than a commendator. However, he continued as commendator when he was appointed Bishop of Orkney in 1541. He was, however, exceptional in that he placed the benefit of the community before himself. Others were far less charitable, quietly working towards the end of monastic life and the creation of temporal lordships in place of their abbeys. At Newbattle, following the resignation of the last abbot in 1547, the local Ker family became commendators, creating a house within the cloister ranges which still exists. It was created a temporal lordship in 1587, by when the religious community had disappeared. By the time the Scottish Reformation had been achieved in 1560, few Cistercian monks remained.

Only one Cistercian abbey in Britain produced an offshoot which is still a house of Cistercian monks, and even there the connection is not direct. In the early eighteenth century, Sir Ambrose Phillips acquired the ruins of Garendon Abbey which he demolished to build his new house, Garendon Hall. This house was demolished in 1964, leaving no trace of the monastic buildings on the surface. One of the nineteenth-century owners, Ambrose Lyle Phillips, a convert to Roman Catholicism, became convinced that he was profiting from the occupation of monastic land, and in expiation founded Mount St Bernard Abbey for Cistercian monks in the 1840s.

Further Reading

1 Who were the Cistercians?

For the origins of the Cistercian order, see D Knowles, *The Monastic Orders in England* (Cambridge 1963), particularly pp 208-66. This is summarised and updated by Janet Burton, 'The Cistercian Adventure' in D Robinson (ed) *Far From the Concourse of Men* (Batsford 1998).

2 The Cistercians' earliest buildings

Hugh of Kirkstall's chronicle *Narratio de fundatione Fontanis monasterii* can be read in Latin in J R Walbran (ed) 'Memorials of Fountains Abbey I', *Surtees Society* 42, 1842, and in English in A W Oxford, *The Ruins of Fountains Abbey* (London 1910). An analysis of the first architecture of the Cistercians is attempted in P J Fergusson, 'The first architecture of the Cistercians in England and the work of Abbot Adam of Meaux', *Journal of the British Archaeological Association* 146, 1983. For the evidence of timber buildings at Fountains see R Gilyard-Beer and G Coppack, 'Excavations at Fountains Abbey, North Yorkshire, 1979-80: the early development of the monastery', *Archaeologia* 108, 1986 and G Coppack *Fountains Abbey* (London, Batsford/English Heritage 1993), particularly Chapter Two which also discusses the first stone buildings. The evidence for timber buildings at Bordesley is discussed in S M Hirst, D M Walsh, and S M Wright 'Bordesley Abbey II', *BAR British Series* 111, 1983, p 30. The temporary buildings at Sawley are discussed in G Coppack, C Hayfield, and R Williams 'Sawley Abbey, the architecture and archaeology of a smaller Cistercian house', *Journal of the British Archaeological Association* (forthcoming). For the first stone buildings at Rievaulx, see G Coppack and P Fergusson, *Rievaulx Abbey* (London, English Heritage, 1994), for Waverley see H Brakspear, *Waverley Abbey* (London, 1905), and for Tintern see D Robinson, *Tintern Abbey* (Cardiff, Cadw 1986).

3 The building of permanent monasteries

For an introduction to the building of Cistercian monasteries in the twelfth century see P J Fergusson, *The Architecture of Solitude* (Princeton 1984). For individual sites, see the guides produced by English Heritage, Cadw, and Historic Scotland. For Fountains, recent research is summarised in G Coppack, *Fountains Abbey* (Batsford/English Heritage 1993), particularly pp 36-54. Rievaulx is summarised in G Coppack, P Fergusson and S Harrison, *title to be announced* (Yale, forthcoming).

4 The development of abbeys from the late twelfth century

Later Cistercian churches are discussed in N Coldstream, 'Architecture from Beaulieu to the Dissolution' in C Norton and D Park (ed) *Cistercian Art and Architecture in the British Isles* (Cambridge 1986) pp139-159. For individual sites see the guides produced by English Heritage, Historic Scotland, and Cadw. Abbey Dore has recently been the subject of a major new study in R Shoesmith and R Richardson (ed) *A Definitive History of Abbey Dore* (Logaston 1997).

5 The Cistercian economy

The economy of Cistercian abbeys generally is explained admirably in L Pressouyre (ed) *l'Espace Cistercien* (Paris 1994) which contains a series of papers in English and French on all aspects of Cistercian estate management. In particular there are useful sections on 'Cistercian Houses in England' by R H Leech and G Soffe (pp295-310); 'The Mapping of Cistercian Lands' by D H Williams (pp311-18); 'Protecting the Cistercian Landscape (in North Yorkshire)' by J Roebuck and A Davison (pp319-327);'Barns at Cistercian Granges in England and Wales' by C Holdsworth (pp353-63); 'Cistercian Mills in England and Wales' by C J Bond (pp364-77); 'The Outer Courts of Fountains and Rievaulx Abbeys' by G Coppack (pp415-25); and 'The Bordesley Abbey Granges Project' by G Astill (pp537-53). The standard work on Cistercian granges in England remains C Platt, *The Monastic Grange in Medieval England* (London 1969) though this should be read with more recent research. For the economy of Fountains, see G Coppack, *Fountains Abbey* (London, 1993), pp 78-97). For the mill there see G Coppack, 'The Fountains Abbey Mill' in *Cistercian Art and Architecture* 5, (1998), and the wool house, G Coppack, 'The excavation of an outer court building, perhaps the wool house, at Fountains Abbey, North Yorkshire' in *Medieval Archaeology* 30 (1986). For the later medieval development of the precinct at Rievaulx Abbey see G Coppack, 'Some descriptions of Rievaulx Abbey in 1538/9; the disposition of a major Cistercian precinct' in *Journal of the British Archaeological Association* 139 (1986).

6 The end of the Cistercians in Britain

For the suppression of the monasteries in England and Wales see G W O Woodward, *Dissolution of the Monasteries* (London, 1966). and G Coppack, *Abbeys and Priories* (London 1990), especially pp 129-146. For Scotland, see R Fawcett, *Scottish Abbeys and Priories* (London 1994), pp 118-125. For the suppression and destruction of Rievaulx, see G Coppack, 'Some descriptions of Rievaulx Abbey in 1538 - 9', *Journal of the British Archaeological Association* 139 (1986), pp 100 - 133.

Gazetteer

All permanent Cistercian abbeys established in Britain between 1128 and 1350 are listed, with a brief description of what now remains. Many sites are on private land, though they might be visited by arrangement. Sites which are open to the public are marked ★. Some others may be visited by prior arrangement. The individual sites are identified to their filiation.

ABERCONWY (Gwynedd) Filiation of Whitland; founded in 1186 at Rhedynog-felen, moved to the town of Conwy in 1190, where the parish church incorporates parts of the monastic church. In 1283, the monastery was moved to Maenan in the Conwy valley. It was suppressed in c1538. Its site is now marked by the Maenan Abbey Hotel.

ABBEY DORE (Herefordshire)★ Filiation of Morimond; founded 1147, suppressed 1536. The eastern parts of the church, repaired in the early seventeenth century, remain in use as the parish church, the ruins of the nave, chapter house, and cloister ranges can still be traced in the adjacent cemetery and farmland. They lie at the centre of a substantial precinct on the east side of the B4347, 2 miles (3km) north of Pontrilas.

BALMERINO (Fife)★ Filiation of Melrose; founded c1227. Parts of the south and west walls of the church survive. The cloister was on the north side of the church, and the chapter house and a part of the east range survives, converted into a house at the suppression. The fragmentary ruins which are maintained by the National Trust for Scotland, lie in the village of Balmerino on the south shore of the Firth of Tay some 5 miles (8km) west of the Tay road bridge.

BASINGWERK (Flintshire)★ Filiation of Savigny; founded in 1131, probably with a temporary site at Hen Blas, and suppressed in 1535. The surviving buildings which date mainly from the early 13th century and include parts of the church, the east and south ranges of the cloister, are at Greenfield, near Holywell, off the B5121. A Cadw property.

BEAULIEU (Hampshire)★ Filiation of Cîteaux; founded in 1203, and suppressed in 1538. The refectory survives in use as the parish church, together with the northern part of the west range and the enclosure of the cloister. The foundations of the church have been laid out for display. The great gatehouse has been converted to a residence, Palace House. The outer gatehouse, the remains of a mill, and other fragmentary buildings survive within the remains of a walled precinct. The abbey site comprises the grounds of the National Motor Museum, on the B3054 12 miles (19km) south-west of Southampton.

BIDDLESDEN (Buckinghamshire) Filiation of Waverley; founded from Garendon in 1147, and suppressed in 1538. There are no surviving remains and the site is marked by an 18th-century house, Biddlesdon Park, 4 miles (6.5km) north-east of Brackley.

BINDON (Dorset) Filiation of Waverley; founded 1172, suppressed 1539. Situated on private land off the A352 some $4\frac{1}{2}$ miles (7km) east of Wool, there are slight standing remains of the church and east range.

BORDESLEY (Worcestershire)★ Filiation of Waverley; founded from Garendon in 1138, and suppressed in 1538. The site is now a public park in Needle Lane, Waterside, Redditch. There are substantial earthworks and the eastern parts of the church have been conserved for display. There is also an exhibition of find from the site.

BOXLEY (Kent) Filiation of Clairvaux; founded in 1143, and suppressed in 1538. Its fragmentary remains lie in the garden of an 18th-century private house of the same name between the A229 and A249. To the south-west of the central buildings, a 13th-century barn survives.

BRUERN (Oxfordshire) Filiation of Waverley; founded in 1147, and suppressed in 1536. Nothing remains of the abbey which was on the Evenlode River 5 miles, (8km) south-west of Chipping Norton, and its site is now marked by a private house off the A361.

BUCKFAST (Devon)★ Filiation of Savigny; founded 1136, suppressed 1538 and refounded as a Benedictine community in 1882. The site of the church and cloister ranges is occupied by the present monastery begun in 1907 and which was designed to stand where possible on medieval foundations. The only medieval buildings to survive are the guest hall and its service buildings in the inner court, now reroofed and serving as a visitor centre.

BUCKLAND (Devon)★ Filiation of Savigny; founded in 1278 and suppressed in 1538. The principle survival is the abbey church, converted into a mansion by Richard Grenville, and acquired by Sir Francis Drake in 1580. A National Trust Property, 8 miles (13km) north of Plymouth off the A386.

BUILDWAS (Shropshire)★ Filiation of Savigny; founded in 1135, and suppressed in 1536(?). There are substantial remains of the central buildings, and the greater part of the precinct can still be traced as earthworks. It lies in the Severn valley, 2 miles (3km) west of Ironbridge on the west side of the B4378. An English Heritage property.

BYLAND (N Yorkshire)★ Filiation of Furness; founded initially in 1135 at Calder, moved to Hood, near Thirsk in 1138, to Old Byland in 1143, to Stocking in 1147, and finally moving to its final site in 1177. It was suppressed in 1539. Large parts of the church and cloister building survive at the centre of an immense precinct which is clearly defined by earthworks in a shallow valley between Oldstead and Wass, 8 miles (13km) east of Thirsk. There is a display of finds from the site. An English Heritage property

CALDER (Cumbria) Filiation of Furness; founded in 1143, and suppressed in 1536. Substantial remains of the church and east range survive in the grounds of a late 18th-century private hose near Calder Bridge, 4 miles (6.5km) south-east of Egremont.

CLEEVE (Somerset)★ Filiation of Rievaulx; founded in 1198 from Revesby, and suppressed 1537. The south and east ranges of the cloister survive largely intact, together with the foundations of the church, at the centre of a large earthwork precinct, together with a fine inner gatehouse. The site lies 6 miles (10km) east of Dunster on a minor road on the south side of the A39. An English Heritage property.

COGGESHALL (Essex) Filiation of Savigny; founded in 1140, and suppressed in 1538. Part of the east range survives as part of a private house at Little Coggeshall. The parish church was the gate chapel of the monastery. In Little Coggeshall on the A120

COMBE (Warwickshire)★ Filiation of Waverley; founded in 1150, and suppressed in 1539. The cloister buildings survive in part within a house of the same name built in the 1860s to replace a house of the 1680s. Combe Abbey is now a hotel, and its park, which represents the medieval precinct, is a public park 4 miles (6.5km) east of Coventry.

COMBERMERE (Cheshire) Filiation of Savigny; founded in 1133, and suppressed in 1538. There are no remains of the monastery, the site of which is now marked by a private house, $2\frac{1}{2}$ miles(4km) north-east of Whitchurch off the A525.

COUPAR ANGUS (Perth and Kinross) Filiation of Melrose; founded before 1154. Only the gatehouse survives, but there are many carved stones from the site in the modern church which is built on the site of the nave and incorporates the remains of nave piers. On the south side of the town of Coupar Angus and on the east side of the A923, 15 miles (24km) north of Dundee.

CROXDEN (Staffordshire)★ Filiation of Aunay-sur-Odon; founded in 1176 at Cotton, moved to Croxden in 1178, and suppressed in 1538. Substantial remains exist of the church and cloister ranges and a detached abbot's house. The precinct is clearly defined by earthworks, and retains a late medieval barn which is still in agricultural use. In the village of Croxden, 5 miles (8km) north-west of Uttoxeter off the A522. An English Heritage property.

CULROSS (Fife)★ Filiation of Melrose; founded from Kinloss before 1217. The eastern parts of the church remain in use, and there are substantial remains of the west cloister range and more fragmentary remains of the east range and refectory. A Historic Scotland property, on a hill above the town of Culross 9½ miles (15km) west of Dunfermline.

CWMHIR (Powis)★ Filiation of Whitland; founded in 1143 at Ty faenor, and moved to Cwmhir in 1173, the monastery was suppressed in 1536. Excavated at the close of the 19th century, parts of the church survive and other buildings can be traced as earthworks 8 miles (13km) north of Llandrindod Wells off the A483 at Abbey Cwmhir. The early 13th-century arcades of the nave are partly reused in the parish church of Llanidloes.

CYMMER (Gwynedd)★ Filiation of Whitland; founded in 1199 from Cwmhir and suppressed in 1536. The 13th-century abbey church survives together with the footings of the cloister ranges. The adjacent farmhouse was the late medieval abbots' house retains its 15th-century roof. The site lies 1 mile (1.6km) north-west of Dolgellau off the A470 and is a Cadw property.

DEER (Aberdeenshire)★ Filiation of Melrose; founded from Kinloss in 1219. There are fragmentary remains, which have been substantially reconstructed. The site lies 12 miles (19km) west of Peterhead on the A950. A Historic Scotland property.

DIEULACRES (Staffordshire) Filiation of Combermere; founded 1135 at Poulton, moved to Dieulacres after 1199, and suppressed in 1539. There are slight standing remains of the church on private land at Abbey Green 1 mile (1.6km) north-west of Leek on the east side of the A523.

DUNDRENNAN (Dumfries and Galloway)★ Filiation of Rievaulx; founded in 1142. There are substantial remains of the church, particularly the transepts and presbytery, and of the cloister ranges. The site lies in the village of Dundrennan, on the A711 12 miles (19km) from Dalbeattie. A Historic Scotland property.

DUNKESWELL (Devon)★ Filiation of Waverley; founded in1201 and suppressed in 1539. There are slight traces of the abbey buildings, particularly of the west range and gatehouse, and the earthwork remains of a substantial precinct. A church was built on the site of the nave in 1842. The site is 2 miles (3km) east of the village of Dunkeswell and 6 miles (10km) north of Honiton and the A30.

FLAXLEY (Gloucestershire) Filiation of Waverley, founded in 1151 and suppressed in 1536-7. The east range of the cloister survives in part incorporated within a post-suppression house 3 miles (5km) north-east of Cinderford off the A48. There is no public access but the house can be seen from the adjacent churchyard.

FORDE (Dorset)★ Filiation of Waverley; founded at Brightley in 1136 and moved to a new site in 1141 The house was suppressed in 1539. The north and east ranges of the cloister and the house of Thomas Chard, the last abbot, survive within a 17th- and 18th-century mansion. Forde Abbey, still privately owned but open to the public in the summer months, lies 3 miles (5km) south-east of Chard close to the village of Thorncombe on a minor road off the B3162.

FOUNTAINS (N Yorkshire)★ Filiation of Clairvaux, founded in 1132, and suppressed in 1539. The best-preserved Cistercian monastery in Britain, its ruins survive at the centre of a walled precinct 4 miles (6.5km) to the south-west of Ripon off the B6265. A National Trust property.

FURNESS (Cumbria)★ Filiation of Savigny; founded initially at Tulketh in 1123, moved to Furness in 1127, and suppressed in 1537. Substantial ruins survive within a walled precinct 2 miles (3.2km) north of Barrow in Furness on the east side of the A590. There is a display of finds from the site in a purpose-built visitor centre. An English Heritage property.

GARENDON (Leicestershire) Filiation of Waverley; founded in 1133, and suppressed in 1536. There are no visible remains, though the site has been partly traced by excavation in Garendon Park, 2 miles (3.2km) west of Loughborough, 1 mile (1.6km) north of the A512.

GLENLUCE (Dumfries and Galloway)★ Filiation of Rievaulx; founded from Dundrennan in 1191 and survived as a monastic community until 1602. The south transept and parts of the presbytery survive almost to full height, though the nave is heavily ruined. The best survival on the site in the square, late-medieval chapter house which retains its vault. This abbey is particularly important for the evidence it retains for a piped water supply. A Historic Scotland property.

GRACE DIEU (Monmouthshire) Filiation of Waverley; founded in 1226, and suppressed in 1536. The last Cistercian foundation in Wales, it is also the least known. Its site cannot be precisely fixed but is thought to be marked by slight earthworks in Abbey Meadow on the east bank of the River Trothy, 4 miles (6.5km) west of Monmouth and 1 mile (1.6km) south of the B4233.

HAILES (Gloucestershire)★ Filiation of Cîteaux; founded in 1246 from Beaulieu and suppressed in 1539. The church and cloister ranges are represented by low walling at the centre of a substantial earthwork precinct. There is a purpose-built visitor centre with a display of architectural detail, floor tiles, and other finds from the site. The gate chapel survives in use as the parish church. An English Heritage property.

HOLMCULTRAM (Cumbria)★ Filiation of Melrose, founded in 1150 and suppressed in 1538. The western parts of the nave remain in use as the parish church of Abbey Town at the junction of the B5302 and B5307, 15 miles (24km) north-west of Carlisle.

HULTON (Staffordshire)★ Filiation of Savigny, founded in 1219 from Combermere, and suppressed in 1538. The site is largely known from excavation, though the eastern parts of the church have been left exposed for public display next to Carmountside High School at Hulton Abbey, 2 miles (3.2km) north of Stoke on Trent.

JERVAULX (N Yorkshire)★ Filiation of Byland, founded in 1150 at Fors, moving to Jervaulx in 1156, and suppressed in 1537. First excavated in the early 19th century, the ruins of Jervaulx were incorporated in a garden, making it one of the most attractive monastic ruins in Britain. The site lies in the park of the 17th-century Jervaulx Hall on the east side of the A6108 2 miles (3.2km) east of East Whitton and is open to the public.

KINGSWOOD (Gloucestershire)★ Filiation of Tintern, initially founded in 1139, moved rapidly to Hazelton, returned to Kingswood in 1147-8, left for Tetbury in 1148, but settled on a new site in Kingswood in 1149-50. The abbey was suppressed in 1538. Its site is at Kingswood on the B4060 1 mile (1.6km) south-west of Wooton under Edge. The gatehouse, all that remains above ground, is an English Heritage property.

KINLOSS (Moray)★ Filiation of Melrose; founded in 1150 and ceased to function as a monastery in 1601. The principal standing remains are of the south transept and the adjacent sacristy, and of the abbot's house. The site lies in a graveyard on the edge of the village of Kinloss on the B9089 3 miles (5km) north-west of Forres.

KIRKSTALL (W Yorkshire)★ Filiation of Fountains, founded in 1147 at Barnoldswick and moved to Kirkstall near Leeds in 1152. The abbey was suppressed in 1540. Substantial remains of the church, cloister buildings, and inner gatehouse survive in a public park, owned and displayed by Leeds City Council, at Kirkstall, bisected by the A65 3 miles (4.8km) north-west of Leeds city centre.

KIRKSTEAD (Lincolnshire)★ Filiation of Fountains, founded in 1139, and suppressed in 1537. Of the church, only a fragment of masonry survives, and the remainder of the cloister and precinct is clearly traceable in fine earthworks. Although the site is now privately owned, it is crossed by a public footpath and can be visited easily. To the south of the precinct is the gate chapel, intact and still in use by the parish. The site lies 7 miles (11km) south-west of Horncastle on the south side of the B1197.

LLANTARNAM (Monmouthshire) Filiation of Whitland, founded in 1179 from Strata Florida, and suppressed in 1536. The site is now occupied by a house of the 16th-19th centuries 3 miles (4.8km) north of Newport off the A4042. The layout of the house probably reflects some of the layout of the cloister ranges and may incorporate medieval fabric. Since 1946, the house has been occupied by the Sisters of St Joseph. A 13th-century barn lies close to the house.

LONDON, ST MARY GRACES (Greater London) Filiation of Beaulieu; founded in 1350 and suppressed in 1538-9, the last Cistercian house to be founded in Britain. There are no visible remains though the site which lies between Tower Hill, Royal Mint Street, and East Smithfield has been excavated.

LOUTH PARK (Lincolnshire) Filiation of Fountains; founded 1137 at Haverholme, moving to Louth in 1139, and suppressed in 1536. There are no standing remains, though the site is marked by substantial earthworks at Abbey House, Keddington, 2 miles (3.2km) north-east of Louth off an unclassified road.

MARGAM (West Glamorgan)★ Filiation of Clairvaux, founded in 1147 and suppressed in 1536. The 12th-century nave of the monastic church remains in use for the parish, its eastern parts are ruined and survive within a country park, together with fragments of the cloister ranges including a fine polygonal chapter house of c1200. 3 miles (4.8km) south-east of Part Talbot and close to junction 38 on the M4.

MEAUX (E Yorkshire) Filiation of Fountains; founded in 1151, and suppressed in 1539. There are no standing remains, but the whole of the precinct is represented by substantial earthworks. The site lies on farmland 3 miles (4.8km) to the east of Beverley on an unclassified road off the A1035 at Crown farm.

MEDMENHAM (Buckinghamshire) Filiation of Fountains, founded from Woburn in 1202, abandoned and resettled in 1212, and suppressed in 1536. There are very few traces of the abbey, and its site is marked by a 16th-19th-century house that occupies the site of the east range and north transept (and which was between 1755 and 1763 the home of Sir Francis Dashwood's 'Monks of Medmenham' or the 'Hell Fire Club'. The site lies half-a-mile (0.8km) to the south of Medmenhan church, off the A4155, 3 miles (4.8km) south-west of Marlow.

MELROSE (Scottish Borders)★ Filiation of Rievaulx; founded in 1136, and largely destroyed by the Earl of Hertford in 1545, though the community survived until 1606. Substantial remains of the church and cloister ranges survive, in the town of Melrose. There is a display of finds from the site in the Commendator's house. On the eastern side of the town of Melrose on the A609. A Historic Scotland property.

MEREVALE (Warwickshire)★ Filiation of Waverley, founded from Bordesley in 1148, and suppressed in 1538. Parts of the church and south cloister range survive within two barns of the working farm that occupies the site 1 mile (1.5km) south-west of Atherstone on the east side of the B4116. The gate chapel is still used as the parish church and is the only part of the site accessible to the public.

NEATH (West Glamorgan)★ Filiation of Savigny, founded in 1130, and suppressed in 1539. Substantial remains of the church rebuilt from the late 13th century and late 12th- and early 13th-century cloister ranges, as well as a ruined 16th-century house. The ruins lie off the A465 to the north of Neath. A Cadw property.

NETLEY (Hampshire)★ Filiation of Beaulieu; founded in 1239, and suppressed in 1536. Substantial remains of the church and cloister ranges, all converted to a house after the suppression. The ruins, which overlook Southampton Water lie to the north of Netley village on a minor road off the A3025, 2½ miles (4km) south-east of Southampton. An English Heritage property.

NEWBATTLE (Midlothian) Filiation of Melrose; founded in 1140 and suppressed in 1587. The vaulted undercroft of the east range of the cloister is incorporated in a post-reformation house, now a college, and the church and other cloister ranges which were excavated in the 1870s and 90s are now expressed as flower beds. The site of Newbattle Abbey is off the B703 1 mile (1.6km) south of Dalkieth.

NEWENHAM (Devon) Filiation of Beaulieu; founded in 1247 and suppressed in 1539. The site is occupied by a farm and there only slight standing remains, 1 mile (1.6km) south-west of Axminster, off the A358.

NEWMINSTER (Northumberland)★ Filiation of Fountains; founded in 1138, and suppressed in 1537. The site is marked by earthworks, slight walling of the church, large quantities of displaced stonework, and the re-erected cloister arcades, 1 mile (1.6km) to the west of Morpeth, close to the junction of the A1 and the B6343.

PIPEWELL (Northamptonshire) Filiation of Fountains, founded from Newminster in 1143, and suppressed in 1538. The site is represented by substantial if slightly confused earthworks to the south of the village of Pipewell, 2 miles (3.2km) south-west of Corby. The site can be seen from the road.

QUARR (Isle of Wight) Filiation of Savigny; founded in 1132 and suppressed in 1536. There are slight remains 2 miles (3.2km) west of Ryde on the Isle of Wight. The site is owned by the Benedictine community of Quarr and can be visited by arrangement.

REVESBY (Lincolnshire) Filiation of Rievaulx; founded in 1143, and suppressed in c1539. The site is marked by substantial earthworks which demarcate the whole of the precinct and the exposed remains of the eastern part of the church, in pastureland half-a-mile (1km) south of Revesby off the A155 and the B1183.

REWLEY (Oxfordshire) Filiation of Waverley; founded from Thame in 1281, and suppressed in 1536. There are no standing remains of this abbey which stood just to the east of Oxford station off the A420.

RIEVAULX (N Yorkshire)★ Filiation of Clairvaux; founded in 1132, and suppressed in 1538. Substantial remains of the church and cloister ranges lie at the centre of an extensive walled precinct, on an unclassified road south of the B1257, 2 miles (3.2km) north-west of Helmsley. An English Heritage property.

ROBERTSBRIDGE (East Sussex) Filiation of Boxley, founded in 1176 'in the vill of Salehurst', moving to a new site at Robertsbridge in the 13th century. It was suppressed in 1538. Slight remains of the abbey are embedded in a private house to the west of Robertsbridge, off the A21.

ROCHE (S Yorkshire)★ Filiation of Fountains, founded from Newminster in 1147, and suppressed in 1538. Substantial remains of the church, cloister ranges, and inner gatehouse within a partly walled precinct, 1½miles (2.5km) south-east of Maltby off the A634. An English Heritage property.

RUFFORD (Nottinghamshire)★ Filiation of Rievaulx, founded 1146, and suppressed in 1536. Only the west range of the abbey survives within the ruins of a late sixteenth and seventeenth century house, in Rufford Park 1½miles (2.5km) south of Ollerton on the east side of the A614. An English Heritage property

145

managed by Nottinghamshire County Council.

SADDELL ABBEY (Argyle and Bute)★ Founded from Mellifont, probably in the early years of the thirteenth century and deserted before 1507 when there had been no community within living memory. Slight remains of the church and south cloister range remain in a graveyard in the village of Saddell, off the B842 on the east coast of Kintyre.

SAWLEY (Lancashire)★ Filiation of Fountains; founded from Newminster in 1148, and suppressed in 1536. Substantial remains of the church and cloister ranges at the centre of a precinct well defined by earthworks, in the village of Sawley 3 miles (4.8km) north-east of Clitheroe on the north side of the A59.

SAWTRY (Cambridgeshire) Filiation of Rievaulx; founded in 1147 from Warden, and suppressed in 1536. The site, on farm land, has no standing remains but is clearly marked by earthworks close to Abbey Farm, 2 miles (3.2km) south-east of Sawtry off an unclassified road on the east side of the A1.

SIBTON (Suffolk) Filiation of Rievaulx; founded from Warden in 1150 and suppressed in 1536. Fragmentary and overgrown remains of the church and south range survive on private land in the village of Sibton, 4 miles (6.4km) north of Saxmundham, just off the A1120.

STANLEY (Wiltshire) Filiation of Quarr; founded 1151 at Loxwell, moved to its permanent site in 1154 and suppressed in 1536. Although there are only slight standing remains, the whole of the precinct survives as a remarkable series of earthworks at Old Abbey Farm, 3 miles(4.8km) east of Chippenham and 1 mile (1.6km) south of the A4. The site can be visited by prior arrangement.

STONELEIGH (Warwickshire)★ Filiation of Waverley; founded from Bordesley in 1141 at Red Moor, moving to a permanent site at Stoneleigh in c1156-9, and suppressed in 1536. Substantial parts of the church and cloister ranges remain within the post-medieval Stoneleigh Abbey. The gatehouse also survives. In Stoneleigh Park, 1½ miles (2.4km) east of Kenilworth on the east side of the B4115.

STRATA FLORIDA (Ceredigion)★ Filiation of Whitland; founded in 1164 at Yn Hen Fynachlog and moving to its permanent site in c1200, it was suppressed in 1539. Ruins of the church and east and west ranges survive, built in the late 12th and early 13th century, off the B4343 1 mile (1.6km) from Pontrhydfendigaid and 7 miles (11.3km) north-east of Tregaron. A Cadw property.

STRATA MARCELLA (Powys) Filiation of Whitland; founded 1170 and suppressed 1536. The site is marked by a fine series of earthworks and small areas of masonry and was excavated in the late nineteenth century. It lies 2 miles (3.2km) north-east of Welshpool beside the A483 on farmland.

STRATFORD LANGTHORNE (Greater London) Filiation of Savigny; founded in 1135 and suppressed in 1538. There are no standing remains of this site, which has been partly excavated and lies on the south side of the A11 in Stratford in the London Borough of Newham.

SWEETHEART (Galloway) Filiation of Rievaulx, founded from Dundrennan in 1273. There are substantial remains of both the church and cloister ranges, as well as the enclosing precinct wall. It lies on the north side of the village of New Abbey on the A710, about 6 miles (10km) south of Dumfries. A Historic Scotland property.

SWINESHEAD (Lincolnshire) Filiation of Furness; founded in 1136, and suppressed in 1536. There are no surviving remains, but the site of the abbey is marked by the 17th-century and later Swineshead Abbey house 12 miles (19.2km) east of Sleaford just off the A52.

THAME (Oxfordshire) Filiation of Waverley; founded at Otley in 1137 and moved to its permanent site in 1140, it was suppressed in 1539. Elements of the abbot's house and cloister ranges are incorporated the 18th-century mansion which occupies the site, and a free-standing chapel to the north-west of the house is probably the gate chapel. In Thame Park, 1 mile (1.6km) south of Thame off the B4012.

TILTY (Essex) Filiation of Rievaulx; founded from Warden in 1153, and suppressed in 1536. Only parts of the west cloister range and fragments of the church survive above ground. To the south of the church, the present St Mary's Church incorporates the brick-built gate chapel of the abbey. At Tilty, 5 miles (8km) north of Great Dunmow to the west of the B184.

TINTERN (Gwent)★ Filiation of L'Aumone; founded in 1131 and suppressed in 1539. Substantial remains of the 12th- and 13th-century cloister ranges, late 13th- and 14th-century church, and several precinct buildings survive to the south of the village of Tintern Parva on the east side of the A466. A Cadw property.

VALE ROYAL (Cheshire) Filiation of Abbey Dore; founded in 1274 at Darnhall, and moved to its permanent site in 1281. It was suppressed in 1539. The site is marked by a post-suppression house on the site of the south and west ranges at Whitegate, now the clubhouse of a golf course, 2 miles (3.2km) north of Winsford and the A54.

VALLE CRUCIS (Denbeighshire)★ Filiation of Whitland; founded from Strata Marcella in 1201 and suppressed in 1538. Substantial remains of the early 13th-century church, west, and south ranges, with a late 14th-century east range survive, 1½ miles (2.4km) north of Llangollen on the A542. A Cadw property.

VAUDEY (Lincolnshire) Filiation of Fountains; founded at Bytham in 1147 and moved to Vaudey in the following year, it was suppressed in 1536. There are no visible remains., and the site lies in Grimsthorpe Park 4 miles (6.5km) north-west of Bourne off the A151.

WARDEN (Bedfordshire) Filiation of Rievaulx; founded in 1136, and suppressed in 1537. The site is now occupied by the fragmentary remains of a post-medieval house 1 mile (1.6km) west-south-west of Old Warden and 6 miles (9.7km) south-east of Bedford, off the A600.

WAVERLEY (Surrey)★ Filiation of L'Aumone; founded in 1128, and suppressed in 1536. Fragmentary remains of the church and parts of the cloister ranges remain, conserved for public display, 2 miles (3.2km) south-east of Farnham, south of the B3001. An English Heritage property.

WHALLEY (Lancashire)★ Filiation of Combermere; first established at Stanlaw in Cheshire in 1172 but was moved to Whalley in 1296. It was suppressed in 1537. The ruins of the church, cloister and abbot's house are owned by the Diocese of Blackburn and are accessible to the public; the west range belongs to the Catholic Church and contains a chapel. The outer gatehouse is an English Heritage property. At Whalley, 6 miles (9.6km) north-east of Blackburn on an unclassified road off the A59.

WHITLAND (Carmarthenshire)★ Filiation of Clairvaux; founded in 1140 at Trefgarn and moving to its permanent site in c1151. It was suppressed in 1539. The principal remains are those of the late 12th-century church, but the whole of the precinct and its buildings can still be traced as substantial earthworks, 1½ miles (2.4km) north-east of the village of Whitland off the A40.

WOBURN (Bedfordshire) Filiation of Fountains; it was founded in 1145 and suppressed in 1538. The site is occupied by a 17th- and 18th-century house and there are no visible remains of the abbey, though it is thought that the quadrangle of the house perpetuates the location of the church and cloister ranges. To the south-east of the village of Woburn on the A4012.

Glossary

apse   The rounded eastern termination of a church, chapel, aisle or similar building, normally of 11th- or 12th-century date.

arcade   A series of arches carried on columns, as for instance between the main body of a church and an aisle, that carries the superstructure of the building. The term is also applied to the smaller scale decoration of wall faces with shafts and arches.

ashlar   Stone which is cut into square blocks and laid in regular courses in the face of a wall.

bay   The structural division of a building normally emphasised in its architecture by vertical divisions such as buttresses or columns.

buttress   The localised widening of a wall at its bay divisions to provide additional support against the outward pressure of roofs or vaults in a masonry building.

capital   The top part of a column or shaft which carries the springing of arches within an arcade. It is often decorated, the Cistercians preferring the restrained forms of scalloped, water-leaf and chalice types.

chapter house   The room where the community met daily to hear a chapter of the Rule of St Benedict, confess faults, receive penance, and conduct the business of the monastery.

clerestorey   The upper storey of an aisled building, particularly a church, which was provided with windows to light the main body of the building.

corbel   A stone bracket, often carved, that projected from a wall-face to support either timber-work, a wall-shaft, or the springing of a vault.

crossing   The point at which the principal axes of a cruciform church net at the junction of nave, transepts, and presbytery. It was the preferred location for the monks' choir. In early Cistercian churches, the crossing was normally unstressed; that is it did not have a tower above it, but from the 1160s low towers became common.

garth   An enclosed space, yard, or paddock normally associated with a particular building, for instance the bakehouse garth or kirkgarth (the monastic cemetery).
jamb   The side of a door or window frame.

laver   (or **lavatorium**)   The washing place, normally placed next to the door of the refectory, but also found in the infirmary and other buildings, supplied with piped water and often distinguished by its architectural sophistication.

lay brother   A monastic servant who was subject to the same discipline as a choir-monk but uneducated and responsible for the day-to-day servicing of the community. Lay brothers comprised the major element in early Cistercian monasteries where they were used to reclaim land and farm substantial estates. By the late 14th century they had ceased to be significant.

nave   The long western arm of a cruciform church. In a Cistercian monastery, the nave contained the monks' choir at its east end and the lay brothers' choir towards its west end, separated by an enclosed space called the retrochoir.

pentice   A passage or corridor running along the side of a building, its single pitch roof carried on corbels. Such corridors were very common, but being normally of light construction, they leave only slight traces.

pier   A free-standing masonry column that supports a major arcade.

presbytery   The eastern arm of a cruciform church that contained the enclosure of the High Altar.

pulpitum   The screen that closed the west end of the monks' choir, either of stone or timber, with a loft above it.

respond   A half-pier placed against the wall-face at the end of a major arcade to support the springing of the last arch.

rood screen   The screen that closed off the lay brothers' church in the nave from the monks' church to the east. Normally the nave altar was placed against its west face. The loft above the screen carried images of the Virgin Mary, St John, and the Crucified Christ, known collectively as the 'rood'.

string course   A horizontal moulding used to level up the coursing of rubble walls and to mark the structural divisions of elevations, for instance at the level of window cills or at the base of a parapet.

transept   The cross-arms of a cruciform church to north and south of the crossing. Called the cross-aisle in the Middle Ages, the transepts contained eastern chapels that provided altar space for those monks who were ordained priests and were required to say personal masses.

undercroft   A vaulted ground floor room, usually of secondary importance to the room above it and used for storage.

vault   The fire-proof stone ceiling of a room. Vaults vary greatly in complexity. The early Cistercians favoured simple tunnel vaults turned in rubble, though these soon gave way to more elaborate rib vaults.

Index

(Page numbers in **bold** refer to illustrations)